# The Sidelong Glance

# The Sidelong Glance

## RICHARD HOLLOWAY

Darton, Longman and Todd
London

First published in 1985 by
Darton, Longman and Todd Ltd
89 Lillie Road, London SW6 1UD

© 1985 Richard Holloway

ISBN 0 232 51652 9

**British Library Cataloguing in Publication Data**

Holloway, Richard
  The sidelong glance
  1. Church of England
  I. Title
  261.1′0942        BX5131.2

ISBN 0–232–51652–9

Phototypeset by Input Typesetting Ltd, London SW19 8DR
Printed and bound in Great Britain by Anchor Brendon Ltd
Tiptree, Essex

# Contents

# Acknowledgements

Unless otherwise stated the scripture quotations in this publication are from the Revised Standard Version of the Bible, copyrighted 1971 and 1952 by the Division of Christian Education of the National Council of the Churches of Christ in the USA.

Quotations from 'In Memory of W. B. Yeats' by W. H. Auden and from *Murder in the Cathedral* by T. S. Eliot are used by permission of Faber and Faber Ltd, and from 'The Listeners' by Walter de la Mare by permission of the Literary Trustees of Walter de la Mare and the Society of Authors as their representative. A. S. J. Tessimond's poem 'Heaven' is quoted by courtesy of his Literary Executor, Mr Hubert Nicholson, and Autolycus Publications.

# Preface

I owe the readers of this book some explanation of the title and the contents. In the summer of 1983 I was invited by the Revd Peter J. Gomes, Minister in the Memorial Church and Plummer Professor of Christian Morals at Harvard University, to deliver the William Belden Noble lectures at Harvard University during the 1984–5 academic year. At the time the invitation was issued I was Rector of the Church of the Advent in Boston, just across the river from Harvard. Peter Gomes pointed out subsequently that he had looked forward to having a Noble lecturer who would cost him only a dollar and twenty cents for transportation. However, between accepting the invitation and delivering the lectures I moved back across the Atlantic, to Oxford, and my transportation costs to Harvard jumped astronomically. The lectures were delivered in December 1984 and I wish to record my gratitude to Peter Gomes and the staff of Memorial Church for their great kindness to me during my stay. The Noble lecturer has to preach a sermon and deliver two lectures, which are responded to by three respondents. It was a daunting but stimulating experience for someone who is not a theologian and who has become, perhaps, too used to the soft discipline of preaching to captive audiences. The sermon, 'Confession of a Guilty Bystander', and the lectures, 'The Mystery of God' and 'The Politics of God' are all included in this book, almost but not quite as they were delivered. The chapter called 'Magnanimity' was also originally delivered at Harvard Memorial Church, so half the book originated on the banks of the Charles River, thanks to the kindness and encouragement of Peter Gomes, whom I salute with affectionate remembrance. The chapter, 'The Sidelong Glance', was originally delivered at the General Theological Seminary in New York City to The Anglican Society in North America. 'Anglican Attitudes' was delivered to the annual congress of the Truth and Unity Movement at St Ninian's Cathedral in Perth, in August 1985. 'Glory Broken' was one of the Keene Lectures, delivered at Chelmsford Cathedral in September 1985.

Why bring them all together in one book? It *is* a book of essays, but it has coherence and unity because it reflects two areas of thought that have preoccupied me in recent years, namely politics and spirituality, and the different approaches Christians have to them. Like many Scots, I am a naturally combative type of person, but I have become increasingly weary of the self-righteous squabbles that many Christians seem to get into nowadays, as they push forward their own sectional interpretation of highly elusive and complicated truths in both theology and politics. I have become persuaded that truth is discovered, when it is discovered, in the *whole* enterprise of truth-seeking, including the disputes and contradictions that must accompany it. Far be it from a quarrelsome Scot to oppose conflict, but why cannot we engage in the conflict with more joy in the struggle and less dislike of those with whom we currently disagree?

I am depressed by the hatred some of my Christian friends show for Margaret Thatcher, on the one hand, and for David Jenkins, on the other. Now neither of these warriors requires any defence from me, each being highly skilled at pouring concentrated scorn upon their enemies, but it does seem an enormous pity that we cannot debate the issues that beset us without resort to character assassination. Christians disagree profoundly among themselves on every conceivable political and theological topic, so I shall spend some time in this book discussing, not the issues they disagree on, but the issue of disagreement itself. Anglicans are peculiarly prone to public disagreements among themselves, but I also think they are peculiarly able to cope with the fact of disagreement creatively, because of the particular nature of the Church to which they belong. Both Anglican spirituality and the Anglican approach to politics proceed by a sort of indirection or obliqueness, what I have called 'the sidelong glance'. It is not the only way to catch sight of truth, but it is one way, and it is a well-tested way in Anglicanism. Anglicanism, to use communications jargon, is a 'cool' medium for religion, and one not greatly given to excitability or over-emphasis. In these over-excited and emphatic times there is a lot to be said for the Anglican approach. I hope this book does a little to commend it.

Richard Holloway
*St Mary Magdalen*
*Oxford*

to
Ann and Edwin Kennedy
beloved parents of my wife, Jean,
for whom I owe them my unfailing thanks

# Part One

# From the Sidelines

# 1

# Confession of a Guilty Bystander

One of the bewildering things about the state of religion in the final quarter of the twentieth century is its impact upon politics. In the 1960s we were told that religion was losing its impact and that secularism would be the prevailing world-view within a couple of generations. Looking back on the prediction and the confidence with which it was asserted reminds us that the only really confident thing we can ever say about the future is that confident predictions are likely to be proved wrong. Far from moving from little religion to no religion, we seem to have moved to too much religion. There has been a dramatic resurgence of fundamentalist religion in many parts of the world, the most striking being the resurgence of revolutionary Mohammedanism. But the Muslims have not had it all their own way. In the West there has been a resurgence of Christian fundamentalism, notably in North America, where it has had a considerable impact upon politics and social policy. There the land is full of contradctory noises, as Christians of rival political opinions denounce each other. Perhaps the really surprising thing is that the same sort of thing is happening in Britain, traditionally rather cool to religion and other ideological enthusiasms. The most prominent element in this newly vociferous religiosity has been provided by Church of England bishops unhappy with aspects of the British Government's policies; they are, in turn, trenchantly criticized by Church of England laymen unhappy with the Episcopate's involvement in politics. Christians, like other men and women, have always disagreed about politics among themselves, so none of this is particularly new. What may be new, however, is the way Christians, particularly in the ordained ministry, have a strong tendency to enlist Jesus Christ as exclusive patron for their point of view. Christians, especially those who are called to

3

preach to others, should exercise great caution when they use the privilege of their office to pronounce on matters of public policy.

Over every preacher's desk there should hang a sign on which a text from Paul's Second Epistle to the Corinthians, chapter 4 verse 5, is inscribed: 'We preach not ourselves but Jesus Christ as Lord.' Paul said it then and it needs constant repetition, because preachers are privileged creatures, raised ten feet above contradiction, licensed to proclaim the word of God to silent multitudes. The temptation to make people a present, not of the gospel, not of Jesus Christ, but of one's own opinions is overwhelming and almost unavoidable. This abuse of the pulpit is frequently dishonourable, but not always. That is to say, preachers can do the wrong thing for the right reason – their motives can be high; or they can do the wrong thing for the wrong reason – their motives can be low. The latter type is easier to detect and is usually found in two modes: the more common is the preacher who wants to be popular, wants to reflect and approve the assumptions of his audience, wants to soothe them, confirm them in their self-righteousness; the other type wants to do the opposite, to cudgel rather than caress, to flail rather than flatter, by constantly assailing what he perceives to be the failings and prejudices of his flock. The first type needs constant approval, while the second type needs constant rejection. Vaseline and sandpaper have their uses, but their range of appropriate application is severely limited, so one tires of the constantly emollient preacher and of the constantly abrasive preacher, because they are so obviously catering to their own need to be either loved or loathed.

But what about the preacher who does what we consider the wrong thing for the *right* reason, who makes controversial pronouncements because he really wants to be faithful to Jesus Christ? Such a preacher may have been brought up to revere the tradition of biblical prophecy that speaks the word of God to the issues of the day, confronting those who are at ease in Zion, afflicting the comfortable and comforting the afflicted. Such a preacher, often in fear and trembling, is genuinely trying to preach not himself but Jesus Christ as Lord. He hears in his conscience the summons of the Almighty to speak out: 'The lion has roared; who will not fear? The Lord God has spoken; who can but prophesy?' Now what happens if his Christian listeners or even a preacher in another pulpit disagree with him? Are they disagreeing with God, are they opposing the mind of Christ? What are the criteria for deciding when a statement is a genuine declaration of the mind of Christ, and when it is just the passionately held opinion of another human being, who happens to wear a dog collar? How do we know when a preacher is preaching, not himself, but Jesus Christ as Lord? I shall be wrestling with some of these questions in this book, and I have a feeling that no one is going to be satisfied with what I have to say. I am not satisfied myself and, at the risk of incurring the disapproval of the apostle Paul, I want to preach myself, because my dilemmas may be instructive as we struggle to find the mind of Christ.

The fact is that preaching Jesus Christ, expounding the mind of Christ and not just some human opinion, presents us with what the theologians would call a heuristic problem. Where do we find this Jesus Christ, how do we discover his mind? The more I meditate on the Gospels the more troubled and puzzled I become: What does Jesus Christ really want? What does he expect of me? What was he trying to achieve in this world? What was his purpose? To find an answer to these questions I have to look at him as I confront him in the Gospels, and I have to look at my own past, not out of any sort of Proustian nostalgia but because I am a puzzle to myself, and Jesus is part of that puzzle. Before I begin that search let me summarize my predicament, the predicament I want to make some sense of, both for my own sake and because it might be instructive to others. My predicament is that I see Jesus as the completely committed man, the man of offence, both in the Greek sense of the word as someone who scandalized people, unsettled them, and in the American football sense of offence as attack. Jesus is the committed man and I am in some sense committed to him, but I am no longer a committed man in any other sense. Politically I am a bystander, a guilty bystander, able to observe, even to interpret what I see, but rarely able to act. Increasingly, I see life as though I were a novelist who does not take sides among his own characters, but allows them a life of their own that he merely records as compassionately as he can. Can a man like me enter the Kingdom of Heaven except after much tribulation, such as a thousand-year stint in purgatory, carrying a banner,

manacled on my left to Eric Heffer and on my right to John
Selwyn Gummer?

But how did I arrive at this perilous situation? Let me describe
it in this way. I suspect that when we first begin to act in life,
we do so in an unexamined way. We lead the unexamined life,
follow a certain direction almost by instinct. One would have to
know everything about creation to account for the causes of
anyone's point of view on anything, but I suspect that people
fall into certain types. In the Middle Ages they accounted for
differences of temperament and type by the theory of the four
cardinal humours (blood, phlegm, choler, and melancholy or
black choler), by the relative proportions of which a person's
physical and mental qualities and dispositions were thought to
be determined. It strikes me as reasonable an explanation as any
currently on offer to account for the mysterious variations of
human nature. I believe that there is a modern variant of this
medieval theory, which locates the source of difference in the
hemispheres of the brain. There are, of course, political variants
of these theories or metaphorical accounts of behaviour, but the
difference is fateful. Politicians or political thinkers have a strong
desire to alter things for the better, to make them right, and their
theories have a strong, mythic quality, a characteristic they have
in common with religion and one that makes them almost imper-
vious to the normal processes of verification and falsification. We
normally know a tree by its fruit, an act by its consequences, but
theories of behaviour and political myths, like Freudian illusions,
are able to absorb all facts and adapt them to their own purpose.
They remind me of Mrs Beeton's celebrated dismissal of rhubarb
as 'a vegetable that absorbs all flavours and imparts none'. I
suspect that most people are instinctively either egalitarian or
libertarian, though each type is almost infinitely subdivisible and
there has been a great deal of cross-fertilization.

I was brought up in real if respectable poverty. There have
always been major moral and cultural differences among the
really poor, and the differences seem to have little to do with
economic levels. In the back street where I was raised in the
West of Scotland, we were all poor, we all lived in tiny houses,
lacking hot water and indoor lavatories, and we were beset with
enormous problems of hygiene as well as by the straightforward
battle for food, but there were colossal differences among us:

some children were neglected by their parents, who spent what little money they could find on drinking and betting, while others were totally dedicated to their families and, like mine, slaved to feed and clothe them. Coming from such a background, where the poor lived in the valley and the middle classes lived 'up the hill', I was an instinctive egalitarian. After all, what reason could there be for the extraordinary differences between people and the way they lived? Even when I was very young, I felt that there was a systemic flaw in society, a structural fault, a conspiracy against the poor: 'an enemy had done this'. Maybe if I had looked more closely at, and asked more questions about, the different ways people handled the common denominator of poverty in Random Street, I would have been a little more cautious in my judgements, but I was not. An enemy had done this, and the enemy was inherited, unmerited privilege. Being then a democratic socialist, I supported the radical rearrangement of society by the peaceful processes of the ballot box. Though I was only eleven at the time, I can still remember the joy in our street on General Election Day, 1945, when the Labour Party won power in Britain: it was mandated to introduce the Welfare State and nationalize the commanding heights of the economy.

Had I been born 'up the hill', I would probably have been an instinctive libertarian: since I would then have enjoyed an obviously higher standard of living and a higher form of culture than the families at the foot of the town, it must have been because qualities of intelligence and energy had, over the years, divided society into different social and economic groupings. Inequalities were intrinsic to the human estate, they were even found within the same family. No restraints should be imposed on individuals beyond the normal restraints against criminal behaviour. Certainly, no individual should be held down by discriminatory structures, but no attempt should be made to re-order the untidiness of society, because history is littered with the tragic consequences of such interference. Edmund Burke argued that 'very plausible schemes, with very pleasing commencements, have often shameful and lamentable conclusions'. And he went on to add: 'Is, then, no improvement to be brought into society? Undoubtedly; but not by compulsion – by encouragement, by countenance, favour, privileges, which are powerful and lawful instruments. The coercive authority of the State is limited to what is necessary for its citizens.'

Over the years I have tried to examine the consequences of the causes I have espoused, and I have noted the way in which some 'very plausible schemes', with 'very pleasing commence-ments', have been brought to 'shameful and lamentable conclusions'. I have also noted, however, that some 'very plaus-ible schemes' have been brought to good conclusions and that sometimes the removal of an artificial restraint on the free action of individuals has involved the use of the coercive authority of the State. Like T. S. Eliot I can discover nothing quite conclusive in the art of temporal government, but I have found enough in history to justify passionate egalitarians and equally passionate libertarians. There is a creative and most fruitful discord here, and it seems to run right through the heart of truth and politics. I find myself no longer capable of giving myself wholeheartedly to one side or the other. So I am back where I started: Is there a place for the uncommitted Christian in political debate? What happens to a person's soul when one can honestly no longer take sides in most political debates because one feels the force of both sides of the argument? My difficulty is compounded by the fact that I am glad others take sides. I rejoice in the theory of nega-tivity whereby the passionate pronouncement of a truth will lead to the equally passionate pronouncement of the opposite truth. I believe there is a corrective dynamic in democratic institutions whereby powerful and popular political causes inevitably over-reach themselves and are adjusted by historic reactions. The trouble is that perceiving this process can undermine one's ability to take part in it. Is there, then, a place in the kingdom of the committed for Laodiceans like me, who are neither cold nor hot, or will Jesus simply spew us out of his mouth?

I said earlier that my dilemma is that I am an uncommitted man who tries to follow Jesus, the totally committed man. Following Jesus is hard enough, but it is made harder for me by the confident way in which people and causes claim his patronage for their positions. The confusion is vastly increased by the quite extraordinary way in which followers of Jesus, convinced of his general support, if they do not actually claim his detailed dictation on the subject, are often in total disagreement with other equally committed followers of Jesus. How are we to deal

8

with this 'discord in the pact of things, this endless war 'twixt truth and truth'?

I cannot propound a confident answer, but I would like to share some thought in progress. First of all, what was Jesus totally committed to? It seems to me that the only really confident answer one can give is that he was committed to the will of God. Herbert Kelly used to take delight in pointing out that Christians are also called to be obedient to the will of God, that one could never say for certain what the will of God is, and that that was the joke. The joke seems to have been appreciated by Jesus. Most of his teaching seems to come in code and parable and exaggeration, exaggeration almost comic in its scale. Where he appears to be at his most straightforward and understandable, as in matters of sexual behaviour and response to violence, he propounded an absolutist ethic that seems unrealizable outside a Trappist monastery. Yet, sinless himself, he seems to have been remarkably at home with the sinful, were they whores, capitalists or tough Roman soldiers. He numbered among his acquaintances both revolutionaries and men who had grown rich collaborating with the hated imperialists. Whenever he was asked a directly political question he replied in epigrams that were almost Zenlike in their impenetrability. His most straightforward anger seems to have been reserved for the stiffly religious, those wholly convinced of their own rightness, those for whom truth seemed small, a manageable commodity, gathered exclusively into their own barns: 'Blind guides, whited sepulchres, hypocrites' (Matt. 23). Then he went enigmatically to the cross, and people have fought over the meaning of his death as they have fought over the meaning of his words. That death is vast and depthless in its meaning, but I have sometimes imagined that I have seen just the beginnings of a clue to one of its meanings, and it brings me to my conclusion. Hegel pointed out that the greatest crises in history are not those of right versus wrong, but of right versus right. What can God do with a world that tears itself apart over competing truths? If Jesus Christ is indeed the Truth, then the conflict of truth with truth must be fought out on his Body.

This is surely one aspect of the mysterious tradition of the suffering God. The fact that we take one aspect of the truth, one sidelong glimpse of the vastness of God, and use it against those who see from a different angle, must surely pierce God. So the cross is a representation of the violence we do to the truth; but it is more than that. It is in some mysterious sense the reconciliation of truth with truth. Truth must be suffered in all its contrariety, its impossibility. The pain of truth must be endured, the pain of opposition, because truth is only realized, its triumph only comes, when it is held together in an excruciating tension. The triumph of truth is in its crucifixion.

So there may be a place, after all, for the uncommitted, the guilty bystander. It may be that God has sent us forth as witnesses to the everlasting contradiction that the arms of the crucified are opened to embrace all truth, and that only the whole truth is truth.

> On a huge hill,
> Cragged, and steep, Truth stands, and he that will
> Reach her, about must, and about must go.*

*John Donne, *Satire* 3.

# 2

# The Politics of God

Allowing for some understandable exaggeration on the subject, I have probably preached about a thousand sermons since I entered the ministry over twenty years ago, and what is more, I have kept most of them. Some of them I recycle occasionally, but most of them I keep for other reasons. Shakespeare talked about the whirligig of time bringing in its revenges, and those old sermons teach me exactly what he meant. It is humbling and disconcerting to read statements – passionate, often eloquent statements – that we once uttered with absolute conviction but that we now disagree with, just as absolutely. Keeping old sermons and speeches is not vanity, it is a private hostage to time and its revenges. How do I know that the positions I espouse today will not be repudiated by me in ten years' time? Any creeping tendency to claims of infallibility can be effectively punctured by a careful resort to those old files. But how do we account for this fickleness, this changeableness? What is the whirligig of time telling us?

First, there is some gain to report. Presumably as we get older, read more, listen, observe, experience more, we widen our store of knowledge, and we become a little humbler in the face of the complex nature of reality. Cardinal Newman said that change was the law of life and to be perfect was to have changed often. Someone else has said that you are as old as the last time you changed your mind about something. So there is some gain to report. But, equally, there is loss to record. As one gets older one's level of expectation tends to diminish. At twenty-five it is still possible to believe that we have time to eradicate all those habits and characteristics that militate against the human ideal. At fifty we can come to realize that change is very difficult, and there is a lot about ourselves that we are stuck with, even though we may not like it. In *Temporary Kings* Anthony Powell summed up the paradox perfectly:

> Each recriminative decade poses new riddles, how best to live, how best to write. One's fifties, in principle less acceptable than one's forties, at least confirm most worst suspicions about life, thereby disposing of an appreciable tract of vain expectation, standardized fantasy, obstructive to writing, as to living. The quinquagenarian may not be master of himself; he is, notwithstanding, master of a possible miscellany of experience on which to draw when forming opinions, distorted or the reverse, at least up to a point his own. After passing the half-century, one unavoidable conclusion is that many things seeming incredible on starting out, are, in fact, by no means to be located in an area beyond belief.

In his most recent volume of autobiography Powell returns to the same theme.

> Alick Dru used to complain that one of the least supportable things about later life was the fact that you began to see almost everyone else's point of view. I had to agree with him that tolerance becomes an increasing burden with age.

To my dismay and discomfort I now have to acknowledge that I, too, have begun to bear the burden of tolerance. I must face the fact that I suffer from the debilitating weakness of seeing almost everyone else's point of view, an affliction that troubled me not at all in the days of my passionate youth. An opthalmologist said to me recently that the human animal experienced two major shocks in life: birth and the purchase of his first pair of bifocals. I have not as yet had to adjust to bifocals, but I have found adjusting to tolerance extremely stressful. Happily, all is not completely lost, because I still find myself capable of an enjoyable level of intolerance towards intolerance itself. The traces of my own former certainties cling to me as I grapple with what I hold to be the false certainties of others. The whirligig of time has indeed brought in its revenges, and I find this to be particularly true in the area of politics, especially as it relates to Christianity.

But just how does one deal with the very obvious political disagreements among Christians? The cynical answer is to dismiss them as simply a function of general political discord: people pick up their politics where they live and work and study, they absorb them from the surrounding culture, and Christians are no more immune to the process than others. The only distinctive thing about Christians is that they have a strange need to bring in Jesus to anoint the convictions that they have picked up without any reference to him. For Christians are no more immune to the fashions and ideas of the time than anyone else, but their disagreements do create peculiar tensions for them nevertheless. They often believe, in spite of the historic record of Christianity, that they are meant to be of one heart and mind on all important matters, so radical disagreements can create peculiar difficulties, and disagreements lie around in abundance.

For example, Christians can very often be found in the same household who are both for and against unilateral nuclear disarmament. They can be found both for and against the enhancement of the role of government in the struggle towards a more equal society, the issue classically dividing itself into a dispute about the rival merits of freedom and equality. Christians will often be radically divided, also, about sexual morality and the role of government and society in invigilating that complicated and volatile issue. In all these areas Christians, like everyone else, are prone to confuse grounds and causes, proclaiming that their own principles are well grounded while their opponents' principles are simply caused by unadmitted self-interest. When we argue our own case we debate about the grounds of argument, the issue itself; when we argue against our opponents we tend to ignore their argument and try to discover some other cause for their point of view. This is a hazardous procedure in the quest for truth, because it substitutes amateur psychiatry or mind-reading for real debate. After all, a man's argument in favour of contraception is not invalidated because he owns shares in Durex. This is an example of one of the things we have to watch out for in moral and philosophical debate, the role of self-interest. It is always present to some extent in what we do or say, but it is not always an important or crucial element in the moral calculations we must make. It is also worth noting that it is easier to recognize it in others than in ourselves, so we should be cautious in our use of *personal* attack upon others as a substitute for debate about issues. We should hearken to

Hamlet's advice: 'Use every man after his desert, and who shall 'scape whipping?'

Therefore, the fact of self-interest, the role of unexamined assumptions and the facility we all have for recognizing these influences upon our opponents but rarely upon ourselves, should make us wary and circumspect as we debate. Herbert Kelly always used to say 'Never examine your motives, they are always wrong', and there is something to be said for his whimsical scepticism. Fortunately, there are many things we can debate; there are grounds of argument, there are the effects of past actions and the probable effects of actions not yet taken, there is the endless and fascinating debate about the ordering of values in the common life – has equality a greater value than freedom, for example? In fact, there are issues in glorious abundance in front of us, and what joy the struggle towards truth affords us – or it does, until we are fifty and the burden of tolerance descends upon us, that enervating ability to respond to both sides of a contradiction with equal enthusiasm. 'This also is Thou. Neither is this Thou', said Charles Williams,* and captured the paradox. What is actually going on here? Is it just failure of nerve, or is there something to be learned from it about the nature of truth and our access to it?

These questions, vexing enough for anyone, are doubly difficult for Christians because so much of our history has been made and written by men and women who have claimed divine authority, even explicit direction from God, for their judgements. For example, Oliver Cromwell and Charles Stuart were implacable opponents, yet each was convinced that he was guided and sustained by the particular providence of God. Cromwell claimed that he led a revolution of plain men, 'such as had the fear of God before them and made some conscience of what they did'. Cromwell's particular brand of liberation theology brought Charles to the scaffold in 1649, where he claimed: 'I die a Christian, according to the Profession of the Church of England, as I found it left me by my Father.' My own head goes a long way with Cromwell but my heart goes a longer way with Charles. Being a Scot, like Charles, and like him a member of the Church of England and a lover of that and other lost causes, I would

*Descent of the Dove.

14

probably have died for the hapless House of Stuart and the Anglican Church, because by then it had come to killing and an end had to be made, but part of me would always have recognized that Cromwell was as faithful to his truth as Charles was to his.

I have deliberately used an example from the distant past to give some sort of perspective, but innumerable modern instances lie close at hand, most of them as complex, with Christians ranged against each other, invoking the same God, before they hurl anathemas and explosives at each other. How are we to deal with the contradictions, and how are we to pick our way through

> this discord in the pact of things,
> This endless war 'twixt truth and truth,
> That singly hold, yet give the lie
> To him who seeks to yoke them both?*

Let us remember that our subject is the politics of God. It is difficult enough to work out how *people* arrive at their convictions; how do we approach this *divine* dimension in the debate, this use we make of God? I have already ruled out one easy solution, which is to disallow the divine element entirely: people do not add anything to our knowledge of the situation by claiming divine authority for their point of view, it is simply their way of stating their case very strongly. That is a tempting solution and it need not even be atheistic. We can argue that God has given us autonomy over history and he does not interfere, does not involve himself; he lets us fight it out. Perhaps we will arrive back at a position very like that, but it is not where I want to start. I want to give God a longer run for his money.

Where then, does God impart his directions to human beings, inform their convictions? There seems no obvious way of getting a direct answer from God or a direct answer that will compel universal assent. People are apt to respond to claims of direct guidance the way Bishop Butler replied to Wesley: 'Sir, the pretending to extraordinary revelations and gifts of the Holy Ghost is a horrid thing, a very horrid thing.'†

*Boethius, trans. Helen Waddell, *Medieval Latin Lyrics*.
†*Wesley's Works*, vol. 13, p. 470.

In a poem celebrating the importance of the smallest room in the house, W. H. Auden claimed that 'revelations came to Luther in the privy', and many would agree with him, while not necessarily accepting that Luther did all his thinking in the lavatory. The thing to note is that Luther's revolution and its revelations was not a pretending to extraordinary visions, new discoveries, novel opinions, but a return to the original revelation, a scraping-off of the encrustations of centuries on the original, fresh painting. This is always the way Christians work; they always appeal to the tradition, work on the basis of precedent, believing that God has left us a riddle or a great code, in Northrop Frye's phrase, that contains the norms, the divine self-disclosures that we need, and that we must read as we run, interpret as we struggle with life. 'Its truth is inside its structure, not outside',* but it is a dynamic, not a static truth. Exploring it is like exploring an extraordinary mind that has been filtered, distorted, refracted through the minds of others, yet retains its own character and power to compel, as opposed to leafing through an instructional manual on some sort of machine maintenance.

In struggling with the mind of God, we are thrust upon the central element in humanity's relationship with divinity: it requires faith from us. The trouble with this thing called faith in God is that, by definition, it has no analogue in human experience, or only partial analogues: there are experiences somewhat like it but only it is like itself. Getting up on a bicycle for the first time and trusting that it will really stay upright, is an example of faith, but it takes us only part of the way because we at least have the bike under us and we have seen other people riding it. The same is true of swimming: in order to do it at all you have to believe it is possible, but we have seen others do it and the water is actually there to get into. God, alas, is not available to our senses in that way. Faith in God requires the elements of trust disclosed in bicycle-riding and swimming carried to an ultimate degree. Of course, just because faith in God is unprecedented, without real comparison with anything else, only like itself, does not mean it is without meaning, is futile or incoherent. It is like itself and can only be known from within its own reality. That is why we cannot get at it from outside and

*The Great Code.*

16

why it is so triumphantly and elusively enduring. Faith gives us some sort of access to the mind of God, but it is not direct access, it is mediated access. The experience of God is always mediated through history and its institutions, such as Church and Scripture, so we never have God in his direct essence but only as he is refracted to us through the prism of time. Thus when Christians claim divine authority for a particular policy, it is to Church and Scripture that they must look, and here the paradoxes multiply.

Some years ago the late Bishop John Robinson wrote an article in which he asked whether God was Right or Left in his politics. By a selective use of Scripture he demonstrated that God could be shown to be either or both. It is true that he liberated an oppressed minority from their bondage in Egypt and gave humanity an enduring symbol of deliverance in the great event of the Exodus, but it is also true that he welded that band of slaves into a confederation of tribes that dispossessed other nations in its search for the promised land. Psalm 78 is quite clear about it:

> He cast out the heathen also before them: caused their land to be divided among them for an heritage, and made the tribes of Israel to dwell in their tents.*

It is true that there are touching passages in Isaiah celebrating God's love for the whole human race, and the Book of Jonah demonstrates that that universalistic love extends even to Nineveh, capital of the brutally militaristic Assyrian Empire; but in the Book of Ezra we find the servant of God imposing the sort of ban on interracial marriage that is today found in South Africa. One strand in the Old Testament tradition sees the introduction of the monarchy as unfaithfulness to God, while another sees the King of the Jews as an abiding image of the care of God for his people.

In the New Testament the same ambiguity is perceived. It is true that Jesus was executed for the crime of subversion, but it is just as clear, from the only records we possess, that his real crime was blasphemy, and that the accusation of sedition was a ruse to have him killed. Jesus was unsparing in his criticism of

*Verse 55 (Book of Common Prayer).

17

corruption, but his worst charges were levelled against the priests, not the officers of the State. Since he said so little on the subject, it is difficult to speak with any confidence or certainty. However, I find in his attitude towards politics a level of acceptance that is almost neutral, a sense that he recognized that these things were important on one level, but that he was preoccupied with another level of reality called the Kingdom of God or the Kingdom of Heaven. We were to seek that kingdom, and one of the tests of the integrity of that search would be compassion for those who suffer, but I find it difficult to avoid the conclusion that his agenda was vaster, far vaster than politics; it was eternity and its demands.

Jesus' case against the cruel, the indifferent rich, the uncompassionate is that they have not only failed to build the Kingdom of God on earth, but that their selfishness has caused them to forfeit the Kingdom of God in heaven. Later in the New Testament we find another kind of ambiguity. We get from Paul an indifference to the political process allied to a strong sense of relief that Rome keeps the roads and the seaways open. The State is there to keep chaos at bay. The important thing, however, is the preaching of the gospel of Jesus Christ as Lord. Paul's warmth towards Rome is in marked contrast to the attitude found in the Book of Revelation. Baffling as that Book is, there is no doubt of its attitude towards Rome, the Great Whore of Babylon, reeling from her many adulteries, drunk with the blood of the saints, destined for destruction.

What, then, are we to make of this scriptural kaleidoscope? Do we just pay our money and take our pick, or is there some principle of interpretation that will help to guide us through the maze, unlock the great code? Many principles of selection have been offered in the past, and it is fascinating to see how they reflect the philosophy of their day, or certain aspects of it. Some of the early Fathers used the Bible, particularly the Old Testament, as a great web of allegories, and allegorical interpretation still has its uses. C. S. Lewis commended it as the best way of squeezing meaning out of the imprecatory psalms, those portions of the psalter that constantly celebrate the dashing of the heads of one's enemies against the stones. Apply those bits to your own sins, he suggested. A principle of interpretation greatly loved by the late Victorians was that of evolution. The Darwinian metaphor of progress was applied to almost everything up to 1914, and it provided Archbishop William Temple, among others, with a principle for interpreting the whole of Scripture, which was seen as the record of a progressive revelation of God to the emerging intelligence of humanity. All the bloodthirsty bits have to be understood contextually; they reflect, not the real nature of God, but the partial apprehensions of human beings of the nature of God, the full and final disclosure of which was not made until the revelation of God in Christ. Again, there is much to be had from that approach, though it is not particularly popular today. The approach that was popular in certain circles after the war was a sort of existentialist one. To it, the historical or mythological medium of the revelation was unimportant and had now to be jettisoned. The message had to be separated from the medium like a nut from its shell, and that message was one of radical trust in God alone as one journeyed from birth to death. You will find that many preachers educated in the 1960s will still be preaching that kind of message today, retaining the biblical narratives but demythologizing them as they go along.

The approach that is in the ascendant today is one that I shall call selective positivism. Selective positivists take portions of Scripture and apply them to life like a party political platform: it is a programme for action, mandating quite specific policies for private and public behaviour. This principle reflects the uncertainties of our time and the anxieties people often feel as they confront complex situations. People normally think of selective positivists as social and political conservatives, but there is a left-wing version of the same approach, though it comes up with a totally different platform. The Moral Majority in North America and the Liberation Theologians in South America, though they arrive at diametrically opposed policies, both see Scripture as mandating quite specific foreign and domestic policies. Again, there is much to be said for this approach. In each of its guises it gets things done, though not everyone is happy with the results.

Each of these approaches has something to be said for it, as have many others. They are all ways in which men and women have apprehended the mysteries of Scripture, of revelation. Using Scripture in these and other ways, they have changed themselves, changed the world and go on struggling to change it. But it is here that something like unease enters my mind; a scarcely detectable discomfort, something on the periphery of my vision, not yet in the forefront of my consciousness. So the conclusion of my argument, if it is an argument, is tentative, a report of thought in process, possibly to be discarded later on but, for the moment, worth pondering over.

All the principles of interpretation I have talked about share one thing, and they share it with much modern critical study of the Bible: they objectify, and they instrumentalize the Bible. It is a thing out there, in front of you, with which you must deal, and the modern tendency is to do something with it, for we are a practical, problem-solving people. Depending on our type, we use the Bible as an instrument for personal or social or political change, as a weapon in the battles in which we have enlisted, or as a repository for our own philosophical and historical theories. In each case we impose ourselves on Scripture, either by turning it to our own use or by importing into it our own theories of meaning and appropriateness. One way or another, we cut Scripture down to our size, our shape becomes the template we lay over the material in front of us, and lo! we fashion from it an idol made in our own image.

But what if we are not meant to do anything with Scripture? It may be a newly discovered continent, but what if we do not colonize it, stick our flag on it, exploit its resources, cut down its forests, put roads across its mountains and tame and civilize it? What if we let it be itself and simply gaze at it, enter it quietly so as not to disturb or distort it, and let its life go on around us – what then? What I am groping towards is some sense that we have perhaps missed the point of Scripture, or religion, or God. Our tendency has been to use them, exploit them in some way, figure them out, explain or understand them. We are an activist, problem-solving kind of people and God is the great problem, second only to Scripture, which is inextricably tied up with the mystery of God. But is that the only way to see it all, the only approach? Must we be so self-referential? Cannot we at least let God be God in the utter Godness of being God? Cannot we let Scripture be itself and not seek to explain it, leaving aside thought for a while, to see what happens? Von Hugel said religion was in essence adoration and adoration is useless, is good for nothing, because it is simply a good in and of itself. Religion is like poetry;

more than that, even, religion *is* poetry. It is simply there in its
own right, drawing wonder and adoration from us, causing us,
if only for a few blissful moments, to lose sight of ourselves.

While I was thinking all these thoughts W. H. Auden's poem
'In Memory of W. B. Yeats' sprang into my mind, especially
Part 2:

Mad Ireland hurt you into poetry.
Now Ireland has her madness and her weather still,
For poetry makes nothing happen: it survives
In the valley of its making where executives
Would never want to tamper, flows on south
From ranches of isolation and the busy griefs,
Raw towns that we believe and die in; it survives,
A way of happening, a mouth.

Poetry makes nothing happen. Can we say that religion makes
nothing happen? I know, of course, that it has made plenty
happen, but is it then religion, or only what we have made it?
Have we not mistakenly moralized religion, turned it into a
method of human control, when at its heart lies only the love of
God; God the stranger, the listener, the one beyond all our
longing, whom we can never know but who haunts us still? At
the heart of the Christian message there lies a discovery, clearest
in Jesus but clear, too, though never fully integrated, in Paul
and Augustine: it is the amazed recognition that God's grace is
poured out on us all, as we are, with boundless prodigality, and
nothing on God's side gets in its way, though we constantly get
in its way by seeking to earn it or limit it or control it. We all
tend to see God in our own image, which is why the English
tend to be more suspicious of this doctrine than most! The
English nurture eccentricity, but they do not understand great
madness. Lack of control shocks the English, and here God
seems to act like a Russian novelist, seeing everything, affirming
everything, understanding everything, pouring his anguish over
everything. That is certainly how the Russian nobleman in
Rebecca West's novel *The Birds Fall Down* describes God. He
says:

. . . the piety of the English is a mockery. They want a prescrip-
tion for social order and union with God means nothing to

them. So they pretend that this is what religion is for: to teach men and women to be moral. But we Russians know that religion is for the moral and the immoral. It is the love of God for man meeting with the love of man for God, and God loves the vicious and the criminal and the idle as well as He loves the industrious and the honest and the truthful and the abstinent. He humbles himself to ask for the love of the murderer, the drunkard, the liar, the beggar, the thief. Only God can achieve this sublime and insane relationship.

Could we not catch sight of this in the Bible, were we to sit back and watch it instead of trying to tidy it up? We see kings, harlots, capitalists, adulterers, drunkards and murderers, scheming priests and paranoiac prophets, soldiers and taxmen, mystics and revolutionaries, all in the dance, going through the steps, circling the sun, catching something of its light. Yet it is the love of God that moves the sun and the other stars, and that love moves in people we do not approve of, cannot understand, abominate.

So history puzzles us. Can Charles Stuart and Oliver Cromwell both be right? Mahatma Gandhi and George Patton were both mystics, one a pacifist, the other a general: did they both have the approval of God, catch something of his light? It is light we ought to think of. It is light we see by, light that makes visible, but it would be folly to suppose that the sun only shines on what we see. I do not think God has any politics, but it is his light that illuminates all politics. All our ideas are caught off his light, and politics and theology are the clash caused by the power of the things we genuinely do see and genuinely do see differently. They all have their resolution in him, just as they all have their source in him, but we only catch them sidelong, reflected off window panes and mountain lakes and speeding trains. What we see in the Bible is a series of refractions of that light, as contradictory as history, as varied as an entire continent. I think we are meant to wonder at it and let the vastness and contrariness of God stun us, at least sometimes, into silence.

We can know God in the same way a man can see a limitless ocean when he is standing by the shore with a candle during the night. Do you think he can see very much? Nothing much, scarcely anything. And yet, he can see the water well, he knows that in front of him is the ocean, and that this ocean is enormous and that he cannot contain it all in his gaze. So it is with our knowledge of God.

So wrote the great Byzantine mystic, St Symeon the New Theologian.*

But is this meant to stun us into immobility, inaction, quietism? What is there for us to do, what is left to be done? What can we do with our disagreements, our profound differences, our hatreds and loves? Enjoy them, celebrate them, for they, too, are part of the pattern of the light upon our minds. We are to bow to God, reverence the light, then turn upon each other, the way we have always done, and argue about what we see; fight, if it comes to that. God knows that that is all part of the impact of his light upon our weak eyes and narrow minds. He wills it, suffers it, for it is the way we have become: politics and theology are what happen to the light of God refracted through our minds. They are inescapable, part of the glory of our nature. There are only two cautions we need listen to.

First of all, we should try to understand that in seeing another's point of view we are maybe opening ourselves to more of God's light, and letting in more light is always good. But there is something else we should remember: there will always be some, few in any generation, who are mysteriously uninterested in what light makes visible but are intoxicated by light itself. They are not likely to be interested in politics or theology, the play of the light of God upon human history, because they are more interested in God than they are in history. They do not say much, these people, if they speak at all. We will find them, if we find them, not only in deserts and places at the world's end, but up suburban streets, in quiet towns, in dark corners of churches. In my experience, most of them are women. They do not make much fuss, but when you get to know them you discover that they carry with them something of the anguish and humour of God. Like our Lady, they may not understand what is going on, may find it all rather childish, but they know something, know how to adore, quietly and self-effacingly, and they know what religion is really about. We may never have noticed them, or noticed them only fleetingly, as we sped past them on our way to a meeting. They do not interest us because they never make

*Oratio 61.

anything happen. They are like poetry, surviving in the valley of their adoration. One day at the end of all ends I believe God will show us that they are the ones who understood. Meanwhile, the rest of us probably ought to carry on as usual, God having allowed for that as well.

# 3

# Magnanimity

I shall begin this chapter by offering three historical snapshots. The first comes at the eleventh hour of the eleventh day of the eleventh month of the year 1918. Winston Churchill is standing at the window of his room looking up Northumberland Avenue towards Trafalgar Square, meditating on the cost and consequences of the war that has just ended. His wife arrives and proposes that they go to Downing Street to congratulate Lloyd George, the Prime Minister. Other politicians and members of the Cabinet join them there. They start to discuss the peace terms. The 'fallen foe', Churchill pointed out, was close to starvation. He proposed rushing 'a dozen great ships crammed with provisions' to Hamburg. The suggestion fell on deaf ears. In his recent biography of Churchill, William Manchester records that while Churchill's magnanimous suggestion was being rebuffed by his less merciful colleagues, a twice-decorated German non-commissioned despatch runner, who had been temporarily blinded during a heavy gas attack on the night of 13 October, sat in a Pomeranian military hospital and learnt of Germany's plight from a sobbing pastor. Six years later the soldier set down a description of his reaction to the event:

> I knew that all was lost. Only fools, liars, and criminals could hope for mercy from the enemy. In these nights hatred grew in me, hatred for those responsible for this deed . . . The more I tried to achieve clarity on the monstrous event in this hour, the more the shame of indignation and disgrace burned my brow. What was all the pain in my eyes compared to this misery? In the days that followed, my own fate became known to me . . . I resolved to go into politics.*

*William Shirer, *The Rise and Fall of the Third Reich*, p. 48.

The soldier's name was Adolf Hitler.

The next snapshot was taken back in 1739. It is of a meeting of the two best Christians of their age, John Wesley and Bishop Joseph Butler. The Church of England was at a low ebb, the common people were indifferent to it, its spiritual leaders were remote magnates, far from the ways of Christ. Bishop Butler, reserved, scholarly, severe, was the best of an indifferent bunch. Then arose John Wesley to bring Christianity to the common people. There was a great revival, marked by huge outdoor rallies, by tears and emotion, by the kind of enthusiasm that austere thinkers like Butler found distasteful. John Wesley recorded his famous interview with Bishop Butler on the subject of the revival, and one of the Bishop's remarks has gone into history and been much quoted: 'Sir, the pretending to extraordinary revelations and gifts of the Holy Ghost is a horrid thing, a very horrid thing.' And he banned the best preacher in England from his diocese.

My final snapshot goes even further back. Rehoboam, son of King Solomon, succeeded his father, at the age of forty-one, in approximately 930 BC. As soon as he was made king, 'the assembly of Israel' came and asked him to lighten the burden of forced labour laid upon them by his father: 'Your father made our yoke heavy. Now therefore lighten the hard service of your father and his heavy yoke upon us, and we will serve you.' The people were led by Jeroboam, son of Nebat, one of Solomon's generals and 'a mighty man of valour'. Rehoboam asked the assembly to depart and return in three days, when he would give his answer. First he sought the counsel of the old men who had advised his father. They offered him wise advice: 'If you will be a servant to this people today and serve them, and speak good words to them when you answer them, then they will be your servants for ever' (1 Kings 12:7). Then he turned to his own cronies and asked their opinion, to which they replied: 'Thus shall you speak to this people who said to you, "Your father made our yoke heavy, but do you lighten it for us"; thus shall you say to them, "My little finger is thicker than my father's loins. And now, whereas may father laid upon you a heavy yoke, I will add to your yoke. My father chastized you with whips, but I will chastize you with scorpions" ' (12:10–11).

So the people returned to Rehoboam on the third day and

heard his reply, exactly as dictated to him by his contemptuous young friends. When Israel heard his reply they answered the King,

'What portion have we in David?
We have no inheritance in the son
    of Jesse.
To your tents, O Israel!
Look now to your own house,
    David' (12:16).

In the subsequent rebellion, Jeroboam assumed the leadership of Israel, leaving Rehoboam with the two tribes of Judah, 'and there was war between them all their days'. The protracted struggle weakened both states and they were never again united. The empire created by David and Solomon was destroyed. 'Reduced and divided, they were less able to withstand aggression by their neighbours. After two hundred years of separate existence, the ten tribes of Israel were conquered by the Assyrians in 722 BC and, in accordance with Assyrian policy towards conquered peoples, were driven from their land and forcibly dispersed, to vanish into one of the great unknowns and perennial speculations of history.'*

Let us suppose that Rehoboam had been magnanimous instead of contemptuous in his response to the assembly of Israel: the tribes of Israel might never have been divided; the ten tribes might not have disappeared into history; the tribes of Judah might never have been led into exile in Babylon, and subsequently restored and reconquered, exiled again and dispersed into what Tuchman calls 'oppression, ghetto and massacre – but not disappearance. The alternative course that Rehoboam might have taken, advised by the elders and so lightly rejected, exacted a long revenge that has left its mark for 2800 years.'†

Suppose also that Bishop Butler had been magnanimous instead of pompous and dismissive in his response to Wesley: Methodism might have been contained within the Church of

*Barbara Tuchman, *The March of Folly*, p. 10.
†Ibid., p. 11.

England and the history and culture of England might have taken a very different turn.

Much more fatefully, let us suppose that the politicians in Downing Street on that night in 1918 had been infected by the largeness and magnanimity of Churchill's vision and had rushed those food ships to Hamburg: Germany might have been brought within the fold of the nations and the whole history of the twentieth century might have taken a very different turn.

Other examples could be produced. Those I have given demonstrate Edmund Burke's great contention in his famous speech on Conciliation with America, in 1775, that 'Magnanimity in politics is not seldom the truest wisdom'. A reading of history shows that, time and time again, an act of magnanimity at a particularly significant moment would have stopped or slowed the unfolding of some great tragedy. As I contemplate the nature of the times in Church and society I long for an increase in the spirit of magnanimity in human affairs. Magnanimity is largeness of heart, generosity of soul; it is the kind of human sympathy that succeeds in loving its enemy and often, thereby, turns enemies to friends. It is seen most dramatically after battle and is not in fact uncommon among soldiers and athletes who struggle with each other, whereas it is less common among those who struggle mainly with ideas. Soldiers are often more magnanimous than bishops, and professional boxers than university professors. Churchill the bloodstained warrior was infinitely more magnanimous than the scholarly and bloodless Bishop Butler. Magnanimity, largeness of heart and sympathy, is never in abundant supply in human history, but it seems to me to be peculiarly lacking today, and I would like to enlarge upon it as a virtue we would all do well to acquire as much in our private as in our public relations.

There is, for instance, intellectual magnanimity, and it is very rare. Most of us defend our ideas and opinions as though our very life were under threat. But that is a strange attitude to truth. Truth is not something we can possess like a cherished painting or an old raincoat, but is something we must constantly struggle towards, and that struggle must be a co-operative activity. When we discover we are wrong about something and change our mind we should not be embarrassed, seeing it as some kind of moral failure; rather, we should rejoice because, presumably, we have come closer to the truth. We should not see intellectual debate as an unarmed combat in which one side must prevail, but as a joint search in which both will be rewarded when the truth is finally discovered. Colleges and universities are supposed to be centres of this kind of searching. In fact, they are often citadels for the protection of conventional wisdom. That is why many students organize demonstrations against speakers with unfashionable points of view. We can all think of examples of that kind of intolerance, and it is the search for truth that suffers. Truth-seeking requires magnanimity, largeness of heart and sympathy, an ability to hear an opposing point of view, not impatiently while we wait to get our own opinion in, but expectantly, hoping to learn a new truth. Alas, it is rarely like that. Many things conspire today to create a climate of passionate unreason in which everyone is shouting and no one is listening, and in this atmosphere truth becomes the casualty.

Related to intellectual magnanimity, and an example of a special case of it, is political magnanimity. I do not mean the relations between opposing politicians (which are often characterized by real magnanimity) but between competing political ideas in the Church as well as in society at large. The difficulty here is felt most keenly by passionate minorities who cannot live with the frustration of not being able to persuade the majority. The opposite of the magnanimous person is the puritan, and it will be helpful if we turn to this briefly. Puritanism is the single-minded, absolute conviction that we are right about something and that everyone else must be made, somehow, to go along with our conviction. Puritans do not believe in tolerance, except for their own point of view. They are usually possessed of a single idea and they live only to see it established. That is why they are such a puzzle and frustration to ordinary, easy-going people. They will not agree to differ; they must have their own way because they know it is right. They infuriate the ordinary citizen who does not see why his life should be disturbed by the neighbourhood fanatic. 'Dost thou think', demands Sir Toby of Malvolio, 'because thou art virtuous, there shall be no more cakes and ale?' Yes, Sir Toby, that is exactly what the puritan thinks. The paradox is, of course, that puritans, humourless, relentless puritans, are sometimes right, and it is their single-mindedness that brings them success. Most social reform is achieved, not by good-natured debate among the reasonable, but by the direct action of the unreasonable. Women have the vote today because some women were prepared to be unrelenting nuisances until their demands were met. Other examples can be multiplied. People abandon civilized debate for direct action because it gets results. A determined minority can very soon intimidate the majority by keeping the neighbourhood in an uproar. The trouble is that puritans, single-minded minorities, are not always right and their successes can have terrible consequences. In contrast to the puritan, however, magnanimous people achieve a very difficult but mature kind of balance that enables them to live with intense disagreements. The magnanimous are prepared to live in an equilibrium of mutual dissatisfaction, while puritans only live comfortably with those who agree with them. Whether it is a church or a political party or a university, puritans have to take it over and banish dissent in order to further the idea that consumes them, and they often succeed because it is their sole purpose in life, whereas their more magnanimous opponents are likely to spend most of their time in non-ideological pursuits such as rearing families, reading novels, going to the theatre and walking in the country.

How, then, do we resolve this dilemma? We have seen, I hope, that magnanimity, mercy in action, is essential to the continuance of societies that contain a variety of opinions; it is also the disposition that can turn bitter defeat into real peace after conflict. A reading of history enshrines it as an essential virtue in both private and public relations. But a reading of the same history shows that it is sometimes the determined and intolerant minority, eschewing moderation in the furtherance of their cause, that corrects great abuses in our society. The abolitionists, the suffragettes, the freedom-riders, the women of Greenham Common, all refuse the compromises of social magnanimity. Maybe we agree with some of these causes; but what about the prohibitionists who plunged America into the bootleg era and presided at the birth of organized crime? What about the theological puritans who kept Christian Europe in turmoil for centuries until they were packed off to America, because they refused to compromise on points of doctrine and ecclesiastical custom that were almost invisible to most people? How do we know when to stand fast against extremists and when to open our ears to what they are saying? These are not speculative questions, they confront us every day in Church and State.

For instance, will the peace movement be vindicated by history because it brings an end to the arms race, or are those historians correct who maintain that a reading of history shows that peace crusades have often in the past precipitated the very crisis they worked to avoid, by destabilizing the intricate balance between competing states? Will the peace movement end war or bring on the war that will end everything? I suspect that neither of these things will happen. We will continue to live in a way that is neither war nor peace, but is a rather unsatisfactory combination of both realities. The peace movement will continue to emphasize the dangers of our nuclear arsenal, and the defence strategists will continue to emphasize the imprudence of unilaterally abandoning it. Since neither side can provide any of us with an absolute demonstration of the validity of their position, most of us will wobble unsteadily in the middle, aware of the precariousness of the situation, but suspicious of the certainties of others on a subject that seems peculiarly elusive to proof. The same dilemma confronts us over rival economic theories. As in defence studies, articulate and learned experts spend a lot of time contradicting each other, and most of us, unless we happen to be true believers in a particular theory, stand on the sidelines, unedified by the brawl we are witnessing but uncertain as to the best method of intervention. These issues divide Christians in their attitudes to social and political controversies, but there are a number of purely ecclesiastical issues that divide them just as passionately, none more so than the debate about the status of women and the new insights brought to Christian theology by feminist studies. Will the increasing assertiveness of feminist theology and feminist linguistics cleanse and enlarge the reality of Christianity and leave it essentially unimpaired, or will it tear it apart and leave it a dismembered corpse?

Few human beings find the right balance between magnanimity and righteous intensity of purpose. Jesus Christ had it: he was rocklike in his confrontation of hypocrisy and wickedness, but he had the tenderness of a mother towards her children in his dealing with sinners. Unfortunately, he did not leave his followers an infallible instrument for calculating the right response to the dangers of the times. He left a lot to us.

Like most people who wrestle with these issues, I am often pulled in opposite directions within myself. I long for the tranquillity of certainty, but I know it does not exist. There is no infallible guide to lead us through the surprises and ironies of history. It is for that reason, I think, that we have the greater need for that spirit of magnanimity, that largeness of heart and mind to which Paul exhorted the Corinthians. The uproar is never likely to cease; there will always be the clash of idea with idea, of tradition with unfolding tradition, of man with man and woman with woman. These things are all part of the turbulent glory of human nature. There is no escape from strife, but we can learn to be chivalrous warriors, united in our struggle to find the truth. We can learn to be large-hearted, magnanimous towards our opponents. At the end of all our striving we will not be scored on how many answers we got right but on the spirit with which we struggled.

Part Two

# To the Centre

# 4

# The Mystery of God

When I was young I was bewitched by a poem called 'The Listeners', written by Walter de la Mare, about a traveller who arrives at a house in the forest and gets no answer to his repeated knocking. We are never told if the house is empty or if there are people within who refuse to answer. The title of the poem implies that there are listeners within, but since they never answer we cannot be certain that there are.

> 'Is there anybody there?' said the Traveller,
>     Knocking on the moonlit door;
> And his horse in the silence champed the grasses
>     Of the forest's ferny floor;
> And a bird flew up out of the turret,
>     Above the Traveller's head:
> And he smote upon the door again a second time;
>     'Is there anybody there?' he said.

There is still no answer, so he knocks for a third time, with no result.

> 'Tell them I came, and no one answered,
>     That I kept my word,' he said.

He gets back on his horse and rides away, and

> . . . the silence surged softly backward,
> When the plunging hoofs were gone.

' "Is there anybody there?" said the Traveller, knocking on the moonlit door.' I realize now that the poem fascinated me and continues to fascinate me because of the question it asks and because of the strange, tantalizing way the question remains unanswered. The house sits there, brooding, silent, enigmatic. If

35

there are any listeners they do not show themselves, but neither are we given any certain proof that the house is empty, that there is in fact no one there.

The Traveller's question is one I have often put to the universe: is there anybody there, or are we just surrounded by spiritual emptiness? Are men and women alone in the universe, with nothing out there at all, or is there another presence in the universe? Is anyone listening to us? ' "Is there anybody there?" said the Traveller, knocking on the moonlit door.' It is a question that besets us all at some time or other, and some of us are haunted by it all our life: Is there a God? What is God like? How can God be known? What does God require of us? These are profound questions, but there is something strange about them. They raise questions about themselves, so that we must question the questions: how might answers to these questions be given? In the case of the house in the forest the lack of an answer does not prove anything. The house may be empty or there may be listeners who lie back, silent, in the shadows of the night. Nevertheless, an answer could be given that would clear up the mystery, a voice from an upstairs window, the sound of footsteps approaching the front door. The Traveller's question could be answered. It is not so obvious how our question could be answered. It is not easy to see how an answer could be given that would be universally or generally compelling. Each of us, presumably, asks the question, but in a sense it is humanity's question too. It is a question we find ourselves asking as a species, and it is not easy to suggest a way in which a universal answer could be given.

There is, for instance, the geographical or horizontal problem, the problem of spread through earthly space: how is the human race at this moment to be answered? There is also the historical or vertical problem, the problem of spread through time: how is each successive generation of the race to be answered? Allied to these problems is the problem of diminishing intensity, the dilution of evidential power. Let us suppose that there had been a time when answers were given, on mountain tops, in deserts, in holy places at the world's end, so that the race was once persuaded and the answer was handed down from generation to generation. It will be fairly obvious that some sort of deterioration would set in, a diminishing of intensity. We would expect to find in subsequent generations a formalizing of the answer and a formalizing of the way the answer is held. Sociologists even have a word for this phenomenon: it is called 'the routinization of charisma'. The technical word to describe the early process of giving and receiving the answer is 'revelation'. Revelations, apparently, compel the allegiance and assent of those to whom they are given; they create problems for those who come after. The content and meaning of the revelation become matters of dispute and interpretation. More important, from a personal point of view, is the problem created for those who wish to apprehend the answer privately, wish to make it their own, be answered personally, but who are never granted a revelation. Thus, an inherent tension appears. We might say that certain institutions become the embodiment, guardian, conveyer of the answer, but they are not *the* answer, though they may be held to be part of the answer or the way the answer has inescapably embodied itself in history. Consequently, there then emerges the phenomenon of religious authority. Men and women come to accept the answer offered by the institution because they accept its authority, or they reject the answer because they reject the right of the institution to give it.

However, ours is a subjectivist, some would say narcissistic culture in the West today, so this kind of robust objectivity in dealing with the question of life's meaning and God's reality is not fashionable. Nevertheless, there have been times when it was an approach that had enormous attractiveness, and doubtless the whirligig of time will bring it back again. The Roman Catholic Church was once the repository of this powerful conviction. As an institution it claimed to possess the answer once delivered to the question put by men and women to the universe. That was its attractiveness, an attractiveness that appealed not only to those who wanted someone else to answer the question for them, but also to those who had spent their life searching for an answer to the question that obsessed them, and who had concluded that no answer could be given from within our system that would authoritatively settle the matter, for it was our system and its answers to our question that was the problem. The regress had to stop somewhere; in Chesterton's phrase, a ledge to stand on or cling to had to be found. And here was this great and apparently timeless system of truths and traditions, absolutely self-possessed, simple, yet infinitely subtle, with a place for the illiterate peasant and the most sophisticated intellectual. The attraction of the Catholic Church of the ages is perhaps best summed up in words that Northrop Frye applied to the Bible: 'Its truth is inside its structure, not outside.'

That structure is much less self-assured today than it was, say, sixty years ago when finding their home in the Catholic Church was something of a vogue among British writers and intellectuals. It is, I suspect, a home that many of those who went over then would find uncomfortable today. Rome is afflicted with the same hesitations and uncertainties as the other Churches of the West, and it no longer offers even the consolation of a beautiful liturgy. Indeed, the over-delicate aesthete in search of consolation is just as likely to have his sensibilities violated at the modern Roman Mass as anywhere else nowadays. The Low Mass, twenty minutes of powerful objectivity, even if muttered in a corner, the very thing that appealed to Hilaire Belloc and Evelyn Waugh, is now something that would set their teeth on edge, with its informal style and commonplace language. Even so, though it is now widely recognized that the Eternal City is built as much on clay as on rock, it still represents and will continue to represent one of the great ways in which our question is answered, and answered to the satisfaction of millions: 'It's truth is inside its structure, not outside.' Its endurance in time and the passion with which it has clung to the answer has a sort of self-evidencing power for many people. We are used to taking many things on the authority of others whose judgement and consistency we have learnt to trust, and so it is here. We need a framework, a boundary to our existence, a ledge to stand on, and here it is stubbornly and magnificently present in history. It has been tested and accepted by some of the greatest minds of the past, as well as by some of the greatest thinkers alive today. Obviously we have to make something of a leap to get over and onto that ledge, for there is a discontinuity between the question and the answer, but once we are over the chasm and onto the ledge we find our feet set upon a firm place. This is the ecclesiastical or institutional answer, and even those of us who resist most or many of the Church's claims, preferring some other answer, are perhaps more dependent upon it than we realize. An example of

THE MYSTERY OF GOD

another way of answering the question may help to illustrate this point.

Some people claim to have found the answer, not in an infallible institution but in an infallible collection of writings, the Bible. Again, it is the objectivity of the thing that is its greatest attraction. It is not a matter of elevating one's own opinion about reality to some authoritative status, projecting one's own ideas onto some external screen and receiving them back as some kind of pretended revelation from a source other than ourselves (the very problem being, of course, that it is the self and its endless circularity we want to be rescued from); rather, we come across this body of material, strange, compelling, highly directive, sitting stubbornly there in history with an enormous power over that same history, and still possessing an incredible ability to explain and change and take over lives being lived today. This is the strength of what is called Biblical Fundamentalism, a phrase I do not like because it seeks to encapsulate a complex phenomenon in the brief compass of a card in a library index system. The power of the Bible lies in its ability to evoke submission from men and women to the answer it gives to life's question and the direction it gives to life's struggles. Again, Northrop Frye's words are important: 'The Bible's truth is inside its structure, not outside.' From outside it may appear to us both baffling and complex, with no very coherent principle of interpretation or mode of entry into its meaning. It may in fact provoke the same set of reactions induced by the institutional Church, but once the submission is made (and submission has to be made to something, even if it is only to the principle that we do not know enough to submit ourselves to anything) the truth inside the structure unfolds itself and meaning is imparted, direction is given. The moonlit door is opened far enough to tempt us to enter the house, even though its strange silences continue to unnerve us.

Even so, it is still possible to owe allegiance to the Bible, to submit to its mysterious authority, to try to listen to its answers, without forgetting that it came from somewhere. For while we can believe that that somewhere was partly from God, or even wholly from God, we must also recognize that it took its form in history, came from a people and still bears the smudge and imprint and savour of that people. In other words, we cannot disconnect the Bible from history nor can we disconnect ourselves. And this is no threat to the Bible's power and integrity. We are redeemed from history through history. History is *his* story, if we allow the pun, in which the answer from beyond is mediated to us in forms we can grasp and respond to. The Bible is part of the history of the people of the Answer, the people who claim to have heard the great Yes of God to their constant plea: 'Is there anybody there?' One of the ways we might hear an answer to our question, if we want to hear an answer at all, is by listening to our own history, listening to the tradition, having piety about our past, giving a vote to the great democracy of the dead. That is something of what Hilaire Belloc meant when he said repeatedly: 'The Faith is Europe and Europe is the Faith'. My complaint against those who are sometimes called Funda-mentalists is not so much, therefore, with what they affirm as with what they deny. The answer may be said to come through the Bible but it surely cannot be limited to it, especially when it is recognized that the Bible is the memory, the tradition, of the people to whom and through whom God spoke, and it cannot be separated from them as though it were a thing wholly apart.

We can recognize, therefore, that some people, perhaps most people, have found the answer to our question mediated to them through the traditions and structures, the very culture of our race. Part of the classic function of education was initiation into that tradition, but that is something that is rarely done nowadays. The atomization of our society has made it very difficult to hand on the story in any corporate or ordered sense. Nowadays we all have to discover it for ourselves, which may be why so many people today are unable to receive the answer from within the traditional, authoritative structures of belief: Church and Bible. Many people refuse to trust the authenticity of this approach to the question. Such people have to hear the answer delivered quite personally or they will not believe. They are not able to rest easily with handed-down answers, no matter how authoritatively delivered. Like Thomas, they will not believe unless they see the print of the nails and place their hands in the wound in the side. They want to hear the answer for themselves sooner or later. People like this can often be tragic and fascinating figures. Some-times, for instance, they find themselves in the ministry of the Church, trapped into guarding and mediating an answer they have ceased to believe or have come to feel they no longer believe. What was said of Jesus on the cross applies to them: 'He saved others, himself he cannot save.' Literature is full of fascinating examples of this paradox of consolers who know no consolation, of teachers who cannot believe, of spiritual leaders from whom the spirit has departed. There are two particular examples that appeal powerfully to me.

The first is from the televized play of Brian Moore's novel, *Catholics*. It is about a remote monastery in Ireland which was resisting the introduction of the Mass in English. A progressive young priest is sent from Rome to bring the community into line with the latest reforms. He succeeds, but at the awful price of breaking the age-old serenity of the community. The abbot, beautifully played by Trevor Howard, agrees to lead his troubled and anxious little community into the aridity of the new ways, and he confides in the young priest that he himself has lost his faith and only stays on because the others depend on him utterly. The young priest takes off for Rome, and the abbot leads his community into chapel to pray. He kneels in front of them and begins the Lord's Prayer. Gradually serenity steals over his little flock as they find comfort in the eternal affirmations of prayer. The last shot is of the abbot himself, his lips unmoving, gazing with anguish at the dumb immobility of the crucifix on the altar, his own unbelief lying heavily within him like a stone.

If the abbot in Brian Moore's play is a good example of that dark night of the intellect that can fall on the believer even after a lifetime of belief, my next example presents a more complex though probably more common experience, more common, at any rate, among professional believers like me.

I first read Dostoevsky's *The Brothers Karamazov* when I was twenty. I read it again earlier this year, thirty years later, and rediscovered Ivan's parable of the Grand Inquisitor. During the Inquisition in Spain Jesus comes, incognito, into Seville. The Grand Inquisitor arrests him and throws him into prison, where he addresses him before sending him out to be burned. The burden of the Inquisitor's speech to the silent Christ is that he had made the wrong decisions when he was tempted by Satan in the wilderness; he had made impossible choices that no one could live with, so the Church had reversed his response to Satan in order to endure in history and bring some sort of comfort to suffering humanity. I remember my first reaction to this mysterious parable: I was filled with the young idealist's contemptuous loathing for this old impostor and the corrupt Christianity he represented. He stood for a radically compromised Christianity. Christ had made no compromises, had conceded nothing to Satan. He had proclaimed a radical trust in God alone, with no concession to humanity's worldly needs and fears: he had refused to turn stones into bread for the hungry. He had made no concession for the sake of popular understanding, had not agreed to brighten up his act in order to catch the world's attention: he would not perform a stunt dive from the pinnacle of the temple. He had made no compromise with the dynamics and necessities of the world order. He would not work within the system to get even good things done, he repudiated the system: he would not fall down and worship Satan, the Lord of this world. Instead, he proclaimed an impossible ideal of trust in God and freedom from all the tragic necessities that surround us. We are fish who cannot breathe out of water, yet he told us we should fly; we are birds of the air who cannot survive under water, yet he told us to follow him into the depths of the sea. No wonder the Grand Inquisitor sent Jesus to the flames, since he contradicted every natural human impulse.

When I read the parable again this year, older, heavy with the knowledge of my own compromises with the world that killed the master I am supposed to serve, I had greater sympathy with the Grand Inquisitor. I found myself, to a great extent, on his side. The Church in history has succumbed to the three temptations Christ rejected. We do not have the nerve or the conviction to live by a gospel that proclaims the sufficiency of God alone. We are committed to respond to the world's estimate of its own needs, and bread is its primary need, bread in all its forms. We do not have the nerve to point to God alone without trying to capture the world's attention with a few handstands and beats on the big drum, because the world is bored, and we must entertain it to capture its attention. We do not have the nerve to rely on God alone and repudiate the way of the world. Instead we have learnt to operate within the world's system with great sophistication. Like the Grand Inquisitor, we do not quite or do not really believe in God. We certainly do not believe in God with the life-defying intensity of Jesus; yet, in the quiet, occasionally honest moments we have with ourselves, we know that were we really to believe in God it would have to bring us to the same madness, the madness of the Christ for whom God was the primary reality. Although they are not sure whether they believe in God, many Christians have become sure that they have to protect people against him. They act as a buffer between God and 'the common man'. That phrase, from *Murder in the Cathedral*, was put by T. S. Eliot into the mouths of the women of Canterbury:

> Forgive us, O Lord, we acknowledge ourselves as type of the
> common man.
> Of the men and women who shut the door and sit by the fire;
> Who fear the blessing of God, the loneliness of the night of
> God, the surrender required, the deprivation inflicted;
> Who fear the injustice of men less than the justice of God;
> Who fear the hand at the window, the fire in the thatch, the
> fist in the tavern, the push into the canal,
> Less than we fear the love of God.

There is apparently something strange and contradictory about the answer to our question. If the answer comes, it is never just as a fact, if it is ever a fact. We fancy sometimes that an affirmative answer would console us, and we need much consolation as we journey through life, as we proceed across time beneath the lowering clouds that follow us. One of the functions of religion has been that of consoler. Faith helps people to endure the pains and losses of time. We all know that 'any comfort serves in a whirlwind'. But in order for this to work all the time, something else in the answer has to be ignored, because the answer, when it is really heard, terrifies as much as it consoles. The mystery is that those of us who live in some sense by guarding the answer, by keeping the rumour of God alive in history, find that we are sometimes occupied in protecting people from the loneliness and terror of the God whose supposed existence brings comfort. Historically, this strange tension has been expressed by the different roles of priest and prophet; priests to comfort and identify with weak men and women, weak themselves, and prophets to inveigh against them, to curse and condemn them for their failure to obey that voice heard high above the whirlwind and the fire. So it has never been more than half a truth to say

43

that religion was the opium of the masses. Those of us who have chosen the role of the Grand Inquisitor, weakened by our compassion for frail men and women, may have used religion as an opiate to help them dull the pain that so many of them feel, but that is far from being the only way the answer has been expressed.

Sometimes that answer has been, not opium for the masses, but a sword in the heart of a few chosen ones, the wild and daring ones who have given up all and followed the logic of the answer beyond the limits of humanity into some other region of experience. These are the ones who have known 'the loneliness of the night of God, the surrender required, the deprivation inflicted'. For them the answer has never been a mere fact, or a rope to hold onto as they straggle across time; it has been the summons to an absolute dedication, that state we call holiness. Holiness, in fact, seems to be the only appropriate response to the answer when it is truly heard. That answer demands, not entry into a notebook, another fact filed, nor even a sigh of relief that we are not, after all, on our own, but submission, departure, a going out as from a homeland in Egypt into a wilderness to be tested. 'Ye shall be holy, for I am holy', says the voice we do not really want to hear. Is not that why we look for God with a sort of studious absent-mindedness, if we look at all, because we are afraid that it is God we shall find?

Do we really want the answer to burst out at us from the house in the forest and tear our lives in pieces? Which of us really wants to hear that answering summons, is ready 'for the loneliness of the night of God, the surrender required, the deprivation inflicted'? The Grand Inquisitor knew the shudder that swept through us, he knew that humanity could not bear very much reality, so he and those of us who have followed his example have turned the deprivation into a system of consolation, a religion, something that holds us together in the face of the great loneliness. If that were all, and even if it were only half the truth, it would still be something worth doing, as the old man in Seville recognized. I think I recognize something else there in Seville and, before that, in the praetorium before Pilate. The silence of Christ had sorrow in it, sorrow that we could not submit to the answer with his passion and power of surrender; but there was, I feel sure, compassion in that silence, too. He knows how little reality we can bear. He allows himself to be pushed onto a cross so that we might be comforted by the silence of his suffering long after we have ceased to be able to listen to his words.

Is there anybody there? The answer comes to most of us through Time and Word, through Church and Scripture, at a second or third or hundredth remove, and we never quite disavow it, though it rarely engulfs and overwhelms us with the wild certainty that marks the saints. The voice has been muted, modulated to our hearing, permitting us to hear other, equally if not more attractive sounds. We keep the rumour of God alive, not as a lion roars in a thicket but like a name we have not quite forgotten but cannot quite remember. Have I heard the answer? Yes, and I have run from it, never quite submitting and never completely resisting. One thing keeps me from breaking free completely, one thing holds me back. It is often said that the biggest argument against the existence of God is the fact of suffering, the sheer prodigal waste of creation, the loss and the anguish, 'the hand at the window, the fire in the thatch, the fist in the tavern, the push into the canal', and worse, much worse than that, 'pitched past pitch of grief'.

It was the suffering of children that drove Ivan Karamazov into defiant unbelief. He was not prepared to try to understand a God who allowed even one little one to suffer:

I understand nothing, and I don't want to understand anything now. I want to stick to facts. I made up my mind long ago not to understand . . . I don't want harmony. I don't want it, out of the love I bear to mankind. I want to remain with my suffering unavenged. I'd rather remain with my suffering unavenged and my indignation unappeased, *even if I were wrong*. Besides, too high a price has been placed on harmony. We cannot afford to pay so much for admission. And therefore I hasten to return my ticket of admission. And indeed, if I am an honest man, I'm bound to hand it back as soon as possible. This I am doing. It is not God that I do not accept, Aloysha. I merely most respectfully return him the ticket.*

*The Brothers Karamazov*, vol. i (Penguin ed.), pp. 285, 287.

Ivan refused to co-operate or negotiate with or even try to understand the creator of a universe who allowed a single child to be tortured, and we can understand his revulsion, but I have come to believe that the only really compelling argument for the existence of God is the argument *from* suffering. I say argument, but it is no argument; it is deeper than that, it is protest, it is opposition, it is defiance. 'O God, if you do not exist, what becomes of all that suffering? It is wasted, wasted', and I will not believe that, choose not to believe it. If the universe is indifferent to the pains of its children, I rise against the universe and impose my faith upon it. I choose meaning. It may be quixotic, but I would rather perish resisting. If there is nothing out there, if nothing in creation can redeem all that pain, then I would rather live the glorious lie of faith than conform to such pitiless absurdity. And what can prove me wrong? Only death, and at death I shall either know the answer or be beyond the knowledge that the answer does not exist. But I do not think I am deceiving myself, for I do not think faith is the final gamble of the last romantic in an empty universe. I think faith answers to something out there, something not quite heard but never quite silenced. That, for me, is the meaning of the last silence of Christ. This enigmatic figure, who has the power of God for many of us, the power to compel submission, ends his life in silence upon a cross. The words cease, the long Jewish arguments, the anger, the tenderness, they all cease, and what is left is a figure on a cross. Some say it has been there since the beginning of time and will be there until the end. We cannot analyze a statement such as that, though sometimes we know what it means. It means that the suffering is not lost, that Rachel's weeping is heard somewhere, that there are listeners, that there is a presence. That is why we go on believing, go on tilting against that big black windmill up against the sky that looks curiously like a cross.

W. H. Auden used to make a distinction between believing still and believing again, between those who never quite lose their grip on the faith and those who return to it again, maybe even again and again. I am one of those who have to believe again and again and again, because what other sense can one make of history and its loss and sorrow? 'At times, it is true, one's heart could break in sorrow', writes André Schwartz-Bart at the end of his amazing novel, *The Last of the Just*:

At times, it is true, one's heart could break in sorrow. But often too, preferably in the evening, I cannot help thinking that Ernie Levy, dead six million times, is still alive, somewhere, I don't know where ... Yesterday, as I stood in the street trembling in despair, rooted to the spot, a drop of pity fell from above my face; but there was no breeze in the air, no cloud in the sky ... there was only a presence.

# 5

# The Sidelong Glance

The Anglican Church became a worldwide communion by accident. This is not the place to describe its history, but it is rather odd that from a national Church that thought it was only arranging its own affairs should spring an international fellowship of churches, claiming a membership of thirty-six million. It has often been pointed out that the Anglican Church followed the flag of empire and just as the withdrawal of empire left behind a tide-wrack of English political structures, so it left behind the Anglican Church, partially indigenized but always bearing the distinctive markings of its origin. It is claimed that there are now more Anglicans in Africa than there are in England or America, but I am never exactly sure of the point that is being made when this statistic is given. The assumption is that it clinches some kind of argument or points to some profound shift in something or other, and I dare say that is true in the deliberations of the Anglican Consultative Council, a new international secretariat that represents the world body. In my experience, however, it does not make much difference to Anglicans in Newfoundland or Tasmania. There still exists a distinctive Anglican ethos, a particular kind of spirituality and, for better or for worse, it reflects the genius and eccentricity of the English. That, at any rate, is what has impressed me in my visits to every corner of the Anglican Communion except Asia and South America. In this chapter I shall try to give some account of that ethos, that distinctively oblique approach to spirituality reflected in the title I have chosen for this section of the book.

One of the most endearing aspects of Anglicanism is its regionalism, its autonomous provincialism, balanced and complemented by a real unity of tradition and style, and the thing that is held in common is the matrix, the source of the historical movement that has flowed throughout the world. The word is itself a giveaway, of course: Anglicanism suggests England and the particular notes of Anglican spirituality are expressions of the English genius, just as Russian Orthodox spirituality expresses the complexity and profundity of holy Russia. So my Anglican perspective on spirituality is a reflection upon the Anglican tradition as it has come to me and formed me. It is not a perfect tradition, and it is not universal in its appeal, but I have grown to love it and feel proud of it, very much in the way a young man with a clever and eccentric mother outdistances his own adolescent embarrassment at her unselfconscious oddness until he reaches the stage of positive pride in her colourful idiosyncrasies and endearing rigidities, so much more enlivening than the plastic blandness of many of the mothers of his friends. What follows is not a systematic narrative or argument, it is not a biography of our mother Church. Rather is it a series of affectionate musings upon her, things I have noticed about her, themes or characteristics. There is a new genre of theological writing at present, with titles such as 'Notes on the Liturgy' or 'Notes on Contemporary Eschatology': this chapter might be called 'Notes on Anglican Spirituality'.

One of the things I have noticed recently is that more people come to me and ask me if I will become their spiritual director. The request always makes me embarrassed and ill at ease as though some taboo had been broken, some protected area violated. I always tell people that I am not keen on being a spiritual director, am not sure how to do it or whether I would be any good at it, but that I would be quite happy to meet them from time to time to talk about this and that, provided they do not expect too much and provided it does not become too self-conscious. Increasingly, I realize that I am somewhat out of step. Spiritual direction is definitely 'in' nowadays and even our more radical theological colleges teach courses on it, complete with in-service training and soul supervision. Moreover, much of it seems to be very good. The code word is, of course, 'intentional'. We must set goals, be intentional and direct in the spiritual life, operate like professionals who know what they are doing because they have acquired the necessary academic qualifications. I admire much of this, and I am impressed by the theological students who come to me and tell me about what they are doing, but it embarrasses me deeply and I know I shall never become 'intentional' in this way. Recently, I have started to ask myself why I feel this discomfort and uneasiness, and I think I have now discovered the answer: in spiritual matters I am an amateur, because I come from an ancient tradition of amateurism – which brings me to my first 'note' on Anglicanism.

I think Anglican spirituality is an amateur spirituality. Let me try to explain what I mean. The opposite of the amateur is the professional, the hireling, the person whose business or career it is to do whatever it is he does. He lives by it. The amateur does it only for love. The word 'amateur' comes from the Latin for love. The amateur may be as good as the professional at whatever the particular activity is, he may even be better (amateur carpenters are often more careful and produce more lasting work than their professional counterparts), but the main difference is psychological, it is in the attitude adopted. Amateurism is an important part of the English tradition, and it is worth thinking about. The feeling seemed to be that life was for living, but in order to further or protect that living, that good life, certain things had to be seen to. No one in his right mind thought that these things were the purpose of living; they were, rather, inescapable concomitants of the main thing. We made no fuss about them, we got on with them, but they were not our whole life. This was the amateur principle, and it is seen in three areas in the English tradition: the army, politics and the Church. There was no trained professional officer class in the British army until about a hundred years ago. Officers were gentlemen first and army professionals second. Their code was the code of the amateur: we had to defend our country from time to time or join a gunboat up the Nile or a raiding party to the Khyber Pass, but the values and techniques were those of the British public school or the great estates. We were guarding our own like any sensible householder, but guard duty was a sparetime activity, sometimes rather fun, but not what life was for: the same applied to politics. Someone had to take charge of the absolutely minimal needs of government – and, anyway, the best government was the least. Government provided those services which were too expensive or too complicated for the private citizen, and politicians gave their time for the common good. It was a case of *noblesse oblige*. The same thing was true of the ministry and the

Church: the soul and the spirit had to be provided for and the Church had to be there, but it was part of the fabric of life, so there was no need for any special sort of training. The squire's youngest son, just down from Oxbridge, could fill the family living as well as anyone and there was no question but that the bishop would ordain him. Army, government and Church were taken care of by the English because they were important, but they could be looked after by any sensible, educated chap.

It may be that the weaknesses of amateurism are more obvious to us nowadays than its strengths, but it had considerable strengths. It was organic, natural, less specialized than what followed, but it produced high levels of success in all areas: the nation was defended successfully, the country was governed effectively, revolutions were avoided, and the Church continued its ancient round. There were great soldiers, politicians of genius and country parsons of rare spiritual depth and pastoral effectiveness. Its weaknesses are just as obvious, and they still permeate the British psyche in many ways, though all three areas are now thoroughly professionalized. Nevertheless, there is still a profound sense present that life is for living, for enjoyment, and that efficient professionals can get the cart before the horse and start taking over: certainly this is the case in politics. British industrial inefficiency has as much to do with the amateur tradition as with changes in the rest of the world, and the difficulties faced by the British churches are partly caused by inertia and a rooted resistance to experimentation. All the same, there is a stability about Britain that has something to do with the ancient British tradition of amateurism.

Even our spirituality is amateur. We tend to think of the soul as a private place, at least as private as our sexual organs, and we do not share the contemporary enthusiasm for opening both areas up to public examination. Ours is, therefore, a spirituality of reserve and understatement. Like T. S. Eliot, the poet of understatement, we have our moments in the rose garden; we, too, have glimpsed the vision glorious, but we are somewhat reluctant to share it with the local encounter group, partly because we feel that it is none of their business, but mainly because we feel that reserve is intrinsic to the spiritual search. We know how prone we are to self-deception and inflation, and we know how mysterious are the ways of God with our souls, so

51

we do not ask too many questions or seek to understand and explain too much. We are suspicious of theories and techniques. We have rarely seen the glory by means of an applied intentionality, but we have sometimes caught a glimpse of it out of the corner of our eye, we have seen the sunlight flash off the ice in the river when we least expected it, rarely when we took our binoculars with us. Ours is a sidelong spirituality, we search on tiptoe, knowing how fugitive and wary is the object of our longing. We are wary of manipulative spiritualities, of people who claim expertise in the ways of God with the human soul. We are dubious about the accuracy of the maps produced by the new breed of spiritual cartographers. In our experience spirituality is not a special department or activity, or ought not to be. It is a quality of seeing, a sort of preparedness, an unselfconscious awareness that the glory lies all around us and can pierce us to the very centre of our being. The more I try to find words for it the more impossible it becomes, and the more I am reminded of Wittgenstein: 'Whereof one cannot speak, thereof one must be silent.' I am not saying that we know nothing or must remain silent, although silence is not infrequently the most accurate language about God. I think I am saying that we are in a garden, a strange and lovely garden that contains a crimson butterfly. Do not be too certain you can catch that crimson butterfly, no matter how fancy your footwork. But if you stop trying to catch it and just begin to enjoy the garden, it may, for less than a moment, touch your hand.

My second note on Anglican spirituality is its sense of place and this, too, is dependent on a sort of serendipitous Englishness, a sudden, sidelong sense of awareness, what T. S. Eliot calls 'the moment in the rose garden'. Margaret Drabble has created something of a compendium of those moments in her lovely book *A Writer's Britain*. Typical is what she says about the poet Edward Thomas: 'There are poems of Thomas's that seem to glimpse into the heart of England, to make, as R. S. Thomas has said, "the glimpsed good place permanent".' One of his most famous poems, 'Adlestrop', catches the age and the place in four short stanzas:

Yes. I remember Adlestrop –
The name, because one afternoon

Of heat the express-train drew up there
Unwontedly. It was late June.

The steam hissed. Someone cleared his throat.
No one left and no one came
On the bare platform. What I saw
Was Adlestrop – only the name.

And willows, willow-herb, and grass,
And meadowsweet, and haycocks dry,
No whit less still and lonely fair
Than the high cloudlets in the sky.

And for a minute a blackbird sang
Close by, and round him, mistier,
Farther and farther, all the birds
Of Oxfordshire and Gloucestershire.

'This is England, seen so briefly, so accidentally, so lastingly, from a passing train: who has not seen it so, and do we not all at times wonder if this is the only way to see it? There is no stopping: the train moves on.'*

R. S. Thomas calls this experience 'the glimpsed good place permanent'. While it is elusive and difficult to describe, I think it is a genuine and characteristic note of Anglican spirituality. For Anglicans, I suspect more than for any other group, eternity, with great subtlety and sensitivity, localizes itself, expresses itself through place, 'the glimpsed good place permanent', and that sense of the sacredness of place comes in several ways. Above all, it comes through particular buildings, churches that have mediated the sacred to us, places of enormous preciousness. We love our churches: 'We love the place, O God, wherein thine honour dwells.'† Particular churches and particular places in churches become important to us, because they have become the place of interchange, the place of 'intersection of the timeless moment'. So important does this become for us that we are almost idolatrous about our places, and often forget that the thing we long for is not in them, but only comes through them. Even so, it comes through *them*, they are the mode of the revelation and therefore sacred to us, precious. For many of us it may

*Drabble, ibid.
†English Hymnal, 508.

be a place that has become laden with the associations of many years or it may be a place that was instantly recognizable as being a place at the world's end. I first entered the Lady Chapel in Old St Paul's Church in Edinburgh when I was sixteen. I had just come off the night train from England, where I was a student at Kelham, and was challenged to race my companion up the steep steps of Carrubbers Close into the strange, dark side entrance to the Lady Chapel. I can still remember the thrill of it, the sense of recognition. It was a place prayed in and cherished, and it immediately invited me in. Years later it was to become very important to me. The holiest man I know had been converted to Catholic Christianity by the same place many years earlier, while a student at Edinburgh University. By one of those non-coincidental coincidences he had slipped into that chapel one afternoon in the 1920s and had been 'captured'. He went away a few years ago, to die in a clay hut in Tanzania, his eyes still fixed on the beauty which had dazzled him that afternoon in Carrubbers Close sixty years before.

Most people know something of this experience, they have felt it: the spirituality of place, the eloquence of stones, elect and precious, mediating the eternal. It presents us with great dangers as well as opportunities. We are more stubbornly attached to our places than others and can become obsessively protective towards them; our love for 'the glimpsed good place' can be in deadly conflict with the need to go out and make disciples, even though the good places themselves can have enormous evangelistic power. I was glad to hear the Vicar of All Saints, Margaret Street in London, at the Feast of Dedication of that famous church in 1983, say that All Saints as a building 'did its own thing', drawing and converting people by its own power. But like any power, it is dangerous. As I have already said, we may be called upon to give up the temple built with hands for the sake of the temple built without hands. Here lies a further danger: many people fall into the sacred soil fallacy, they confine God to the place where they have known him best or most powerfully, and they lose him in exile, when they are carried off to the waters of Babylon: how can they sing the Lord's song in a strange land (Psalm 137:1)?

An aspect of the significance of place to our spirituality is our attachment to particular forms of worship. The Prayer Book is a place of exchange, a point of intersection, and it, too, becomes loaded with sacred associations. Everything that has been said about the importance of place can be applied to it: it is both opportunity and risk, revelation and snare. Since ours is a spirituality of form and substance, the form can be the place where we meet God or bow down to an idol. The safest guide along this narrow and precipitous pathway is Charles Williams's famous paradox: 'This also is Thou. Neither is this Thou.' There are two kinds of heretic, therefore: those who limit God to the holy place, be it book or temple; and those who deny God's presence in the holy place, be it book or temple. The truth is always in the paradox, the sidelong glance, the indirection: 'This also is Thou. Neither is this Thou.'

The final aspect of the significance of place to our spirituality is the importance of beauty. I would prefer to use the archaic word 'comeliness' to describe what I mean. Comeliness suggests to me decency and order and quiet beauty. It has nothing of the wildness of great beauty, fated beauty, the kind of beauty that traps and overwhelms. We like our beauty accessible, purged of terror and fascination, comely, rather like that June afternoon in Adlestrop. It is true that some of us have experimented with the baroque and the rococo, that there are Anglican exotics who preen themselves like peacocks, but it is not the main tradition. We are a fastidious people. Try as we might, we cannot get used to bleeding statues and plastic flowers. We lack a certain redemptive vulgarity, which limits our appeal. Some of us manage to achieve it unselfconsciously, but most of us are fatally selfconscious when we try it, and it convinces no one. My own view, however, is that real beauty is democratic and unites, while the shoddy exploits and divides. Dostoevsky said that the world would be redeemed by beauty, so I do not think we should be too quick to abandon our conviction that God is to be worshipped in the holiness of beauty.

A separate but related note in Anglican spirituality is our care for language, literateness. The Anglican tradition in prayer has not made its greatest contribution by means of the science of mysticism or profound psychological understanding of the soul, but by means of language, by prayers of economy and beauty. Language, not ecstasy, is our medium. We treasure the sound of words, following meetly upon each other, and this affection for sound has led to the creation of Anglican Church music, in my biased view the most complete and sustained marriage of words and music in any tradition. The Prayer Book is the best example, but not the only one, of our love of language. We have been a people who have crafted out beautiful prayers. I think of Eric Milner White's *My God My Glory* in our own time, as well as the extraordinary prayers of Lancelot Andrewes in an earlier era. Whenever I read the exhortation that comes before the *Festival of Carols and Nine Lessons*, written by Archbishop Benson, I become newly aware of the great tradition of beautiful utterance as a vehicle of the spirit. That part of the tradition is under some strain today. Whatever their other merits, few of the new Anglican Prayer Books achieve any distinction of language, with the exception, I think, of the American Prayer Book of 1979. It is a book of which the American Church can be proud. For all its occasional infelicities, it maintains with great brightness and vigour much of the ancient Anglican tradition of loveliness in language as a vehicle of the spirit.

Finally, I believe that Anglican spirituality is, above all, a lay spirituality. This has undoubtedly something to do with the amateur tradition, but it has other roots as well. We have not thought of our clergy as there to pray instead of us but with us. Many of our most mature spiritual teachers have been members of the laity. We can all think of our own favourites, but here I will mention only C. S. Lewis, Charles Williams, Evelyn Underhill and, in a mysteriously contemporary way, the novelist Barbara Pym. The lay tradition often affects our clergy, making some of the best of them nervous of professional clericalism. This lay tradition lends a certain tolerance and modesty to our spirituality, purges it of absolutism, makes it accessible to men and women who live up suburban back streets and in small towns. That is why I treasure Evelyn Underhill's comment, made while discussing the years when she had wrestled with a strong desire to join the wildly attractive absolutism of the Church of Rome. She observed ruefully that while the Anglican Church might not be the City of God, it was a respectable suburb thereof, and she would stick to it. I tend to think of the Anglican Church as a tolerant, wistful, middle-aged lady, of considerable beauty and distinction, who never quite lets her hair down. She exasperates me, but I love her dearly, and I will stick with her till death do us part.

# 6

## Anglican Attitudes

Groucho Marx once wrote to the secretary of a club to which he belonged: 'Please accept my resignation. I don't want to belong to any club that will accept me as a member.' He could surely have found a home in the Anglican Church, an elusive and ambiguous body that is quite used to its members practising the curious gymnastic feat of what we might call internal disaffiliation, of retaining membership of a Church they repudiate and disapprove of. Even Marx's quixotic integrity would not have been violated by Anglicanism. He could have left and stayed at the same time, just like many other members of the oddest club in Christendom. However, had Groucho Marx joined the Anglican Church he would also have noticed that many people actually do leave it or threaten to leave it, not because they do not want to belong to a body that would accept them as members, but because it accepts others of whom they disapprove. So there are two curious things to note about Anglicanism. In the first place, it seems to promote the phenomenon of internal exile, of being in but not entirely of the body. Secondly, it seems to produce a disproportionate number of people who leave it, dramatically, in a wave of publicity because it has not measured up to their standards of belief or behaviour. More people seem to walk out of Anglicanism, banging the door very loudly behind them, than out of any other Church. Of course, people are lapsing and changing their affiliations everywhere, but there is something about Anglicanism that seems to promote the need for the outraged public gesture, the theatrical denunciation, or the more-in-sorrow-than-in-anger ploy, carefully orchestrated before the eye of the world or at least the communications media.

Most of the people who leave us seem to depart for Rome, but that may be a false perception, because we know that many evangelicals are put under strong pressure from time to time to leave a Church that is as doctrinally impure as Anglicanism. The people who insist on staying are even more puzzling. Part of the anguish of being an Anglican, for many people, is uncertainty about whether the Church still officially believes what they believe, or whether there has been a subtle process of erosion at work that has quietly removed all the old landmarks and signposts. But there have always been one or two eccentrics in every generation who puzzle the faithful by loudly proclaiming that they have ceased to believe anything, yet who insist on remaining within the enclosure of faith and continue to lead worship of One in whom they no longer believe and of whom they have taken leave with such dramatic certainty. There can be little doubt that Groucho Marx would have been entranced by the contradictions and contortions of such a Church. Indeed, it might even be held true that only Anglicanism could have provided the perfect vehicle for his genius. Apart from its obvious comic value, therefore, how can the continued existence of such a body be justified and how can we account for its peculiarities? I would like to offer some kind of personal response to that question and I shall begin with a private reminiscence.

The year 1960 was the four-hundredth anniversary of the Scottish Reformation. At the time of the celebrations I was a curate in Glasgow and I can well remember the confusion I felt. The celebrations occurred towards the end of the great ecumenical ice-age between the Roman Catholic Church and the rest of us, but the atmosphere was still rather chilly. The Catholic Church obviously held aloof from the celebrations, while the Presbyterian Church of Scotland just as obviously pulled out all the stops in a great blast of thanksgiving. The Scottish Episcopalians hopped from one foot to the other! There were some who wanted to have nothing to do with the celebrations, holding that the Reformation was an unmitigated tragedy; while others, proud of their Protestant heritage, thought that the Episcopal Church was churlish to hang back from the national thanksgiving. Characteristically, our response to the situation was an oxymoron: in our anniversary services we either gave thanks penitently or we repented thankfully. At St Mary's Cathedral in Glasgow Archbishop Michael Ramsey was preaching. I cannot remember his sermon, but I do remember his text and the way he delivered it: 'Fear not, little flock; it is your Father's good pleasure to give you the kingdom', he said with enormous tenderness, sensing our ambivalence, our discomfort at being caught between a rock and a hard place, as we sat uneasily between the two great churches of Scotland. I remember being peculiarly ambivalent myself. I was fascinated by the Roman Catholic Church – at one point I had come close to joining it – but I had many friends in the Presbyterian Church and I deeply admired its definitional clarity and the way it undoubtedly had grown to reflect and represent the spirit of the nation. Theologically, I was pulled both ways: I regretted the shattering of the unity of Christendom and I still held myself to be a Catholic, in continuity with the Church of the ages; on the other hand, in many ways I was a child of the Reformation and belonged to a Church that still bore the imprint of that era.

My dilemma was a perfect example of classical Anglican schizophrenia, though we often give it milder names. For example, we describe ourselves as a 'bridge' Church, spanning the gulf between Rome and Geneva. But people who use this term often seem to forget the nature of a bridge: it actually sits on both sides of a divide at once and is not mystically suspended midway between them. Anglicanism is schizophrenic because it really does contain within itself all the theological contradictions there are, especially those between the Reformation and the Catholic Church. It is sometimes pointed out, for instance, that the Anglican Church has a Catholic Ordinal and Protestant Articles of Religion: our retention of the ancient orders of bishops, priests and deacons stressing the continuity with the past, while The Thirty-nine Articles reflect the theological disputes of the day and suggest a strong Calvinist influence. Of course, these tensions are not felt by everyone in the Anglican Church, and it is here we should take note of an important characteristic of Anglicanism. The tensions inherent in Anglican comprehensiveness surface mainly on the national or international level. They may surface at the General Synod, but they are less likely to surface at the local level, unless a new priest comes along who wants to shift a parish from one type of Anglicanism to another. For the most part, however, the various traditions within the Church tend to live in hermetically sealed enclaves, whether it be a parish, a diocese or a whole province. One rarely finds the full range of Anglican possibility expressed in a person or even in a parish. Individuals tend to locate themselves somewhere on the Anglican continuum, but they find it uncomfortable to try to occupy more than one notch at a time, let alone stretch across the whole experience. This gives rise to an intriguing phenomenon that makes Anglicanism's fabled comprehensiveness somewhat suspect.

It is undoubtedly true that Anglicanism is comprehensive in the sense that it contains within its slack embrace Catholics whose worship and theology is indistinguishable from Rome's, and Calvinists who would be at home in any of the churches affiliated to the Alliance of Evangelical Churches. Neither of these groups has any real contact with the other. Each has its own theological colleges and its own institutional sub-culture. In fact, to all intents and purposes they belong to different Churches, one group thinking of itself as fully Catholic, untainted by any tincture of Protestantism, while the other group thinks of itself as fully Protestant and adheres to a theology that is reluctant to apply the epithet 'Christian' to any group that does not accept its own stringent criteria of belief.

Deeply suspected by both these groups is a third group, in many ways in the ascendant among the leaders of the Church and usually thought of as the Liberal Establishment, though it might be better to call them Laodiceans, after the church in Asia excoriated by the enthusiast who wrote the Book of Revelation. (It will be remembered that he desired to spew that lukewarm church out of his mouth, because it was neither cold nor hot.) On first viewing, this third group appears to be a genuinely Anglican mix, comprehensively absorbing something of the flavour of the other two groups. It eschews the more extreme liturgical practices of the Catholic fringe, though it is happy to wear some of the badges of its allegiance. It rather enjoys, for example, getting into eucharistic vestments, a grave lapse in the eyes of the Evangelicals, while its functionalist view of the ordained ministry is, in fact, closer to their Protestant view. But the irony is more than a mere matter of wearing the symbols of an order whose authority they question. It is largely from this group that the episcopate is recruited and its members are usually keen to offer themselves for that demanding ministry, so we have the additional irony of the eager assumption and exercise of an authority by the very men who are most likely to question its validity and relevance. It may be, of course, that institutional leadership in the Church is the obvious refuge for those who have lost faith in its less tangible purposes. So, while this group appears to have something in common with the others it is, in reality, just as discrete. The other two groups are made up of enthusiasts firmly entrenched in their mutually exclusive beliefs, while the third group is mainly characterized by its doubts and the disdain it feels for what it holds to be the false certainties of others.

It would immediately appear, therefore, that Anglicanism's fabled comprehensiveness is somewhat dubious. Is there a genuine principle of unity that transcends the obvious differences within Anglicanism, or is our comprehensiveness spurious, a mere accidental aggregate of disputing factions? In attempting to answer that question it will help if we can discover some of the assumptions behind each of the three discrete groupings.

Richard Hooker (1553–1600) is commonly regarded as the principal intellectual architect of the Anglican theological tradition. No man did more than he to explain Anglicans to themselves and to others. His most important single contribution was to affirm the Anglican tradition as that of a threefold cord not quickly broken, of Scripture, Tradition and Reason. He emphasized the nature of God as the Eternal Reason that expressed itself in the laws of the universe. Our reason is the main instrument by which we gain knowledge of God. It is by reason that we are able to understand the revelation God has given of himself in Scripture, because Scripture is not self-evidencing: its interpretation is left to the Church, which has been divinely guided to speak its mind in Councils. Scripture, therefore, is not 'the only rule of all things which in this life may be done by men'.

Whatsoever either men on earth, or the Angels of heaven do know, it is as a drop of that unemptiable fountaine of wisdom, which wisdom hath diversly imparted her treasures unto the world. As her wayes are of sundry kindes, so her maner of teaching is not meerely one and the same. Some things she openeth by the sacred books of Scriptures; some things by the glorious works of nature; with some things she inspireth them

61

from above by spiritual influence, in some things she leadeth and trayneth them only by worldly experience and practice. We may not so in any one speciall kind admire her that we disgrace her in any other, but let all her wayes be according unto their place and degree adored.*

While it is undoubtedly true that Hooker set forth the comprehensive character of official Anglicanism, Anglicanism in its perfect or abstract state as it were, it is probably true to say that the abstraction has rarely been perfectly expressed in real flesh-and-blood Anglicans. What we are more likely to find are the three elements of the synthesis separated into factions or parties, all bearing witness to their own perspective and rarely showing much understanding of, or sympathy with, the others. What are the several characteristics of each group?

The biblicist element in Anglicanism rightly stresses revelation as the primary root of the Christian faith. One of the things that made Christianity folly to the sophisticated was its claim to revealed truth. The early Church was not a debating society to further the discussion of religious questions. It claimed a quite specific revelation from God, a break in the system of human religious thought and searching. It was this concreteness that scandalized the philosophers of the ancient world who were always game for a frank discussion on the meaning of life but who could not understand the specificity and particularity of the Christian claim. By definition a revelation cannot be empirically verified, scientifically tested, proved by experiment. That is not to say that it is not reasonable to believe it; it is to say that, to a very great extent, it always begs its own question, it always authenticates itself to those who are called, but it is always something other than they are, something from beyond, an intrusion, a divine initiative, a disclosure that has authority because it is held to come from God. The appropriate response to a divine disclosure is not a sage nodding of the head in agreement, or a scratching of the head while more enlightenment is sought, but a falling to the knees in obedience and adoration. What is offered in and through that revelation is a relationship with the person of Christ, who is both the herald and the news he brings.

*Of the Laws of Ecclesiastical Politie* ii, 1:4.

Bible Christians are often accused of bibliolatry, of worshipping a book, but the accusation is hardly fair. The book is the inseparable medium of the revelation, but it is the Living Christ they seek to know and proclaim. Since they have encountered Christ through the medium of Scripture they conceive an enormous reverence for it. It is inevitable that they should sometimes confuse the medium with the message, the vehicle with what it conveys, but it is easier to avoid that in the abstract than in the midst of the passionate wrestlings of faith. It ought to be obvious that the scene or place of a theophany will itself become hallowed in the minds of those to whom the disclosure was made. In the same way a building, hallowed by the prayer of centuries and the associations of generations, will become holy and untouchable in the eyes of those who have learnt something of God in it. Religious experience breeds an obvious and unavoidable conservatism in its adherents. It is a perfectly natural and human thing. I have known a widow who kept her husband's favourite fireside chair exactly as and where he left it, with his pipe rack beside it and one pipe in the ashtray, put there after his last smoke. The place had become hallowed by memory. So it is not surprising that those who have found Christ through Scripture should treat it with an even greater reverence and should want to leave it untouched and largely uninterpreted. It is enough for them that Christ has met them through it. It seems beside the point that the Scriptures had a purely human history, that they came from somewhere, through the activity of human beings, just as it seems beside the point that the chair and the pipe rack were bought round the corner in the local shopping centre. What really matters is that they have become places of encounter, points of entry, and will be forever hallowed by the memory of the experience. This is why so much of the debate about the historical nature of Scripture is beside the point. Many biblical critics are like excavators dismantling a shrine and dating its bricks to try to discover its genius. Their operation is essentially a post-mortem, presupposing the death of the thing they examine. They certainly provide us with interesting information, just as the pathologist does, but the clinical dissection of a body cannot introduce us to the spirit that inhabits it. Nor, indeed, does an historical investigation of the medium of the revelation necessarily nullify the revelation, as many evangelical scholars will testify. Scripture is the normative record of the Church's original encounter with the revelation of God in Christ, and it is still one of the primary means of that continued encounter. It has all the ambiguity of any sacrament, any material instrumentality that God has chosen as a medium of revelation, and while it is important to remember that *it* is not God though God comes through it, we must also remember that God comes through *it*.

The major limitation of biblicism is that it seems to suggest, when it does not say it directly, that God's guidance and revelation are limited to Scripture. To use an astronomical metaphor, the biblicist supports 'the big bang' theory of revelation: God's creative activity was all back in the past and is only to be located in the past, and only what can be found explicitly stated in the past is to be followed. That was the approach of the Puritans whom Richard Hooker opposed. For Hooker this was an unwarranted limitation upon the ways of God's wisdom: 'We may not so in any one speciall kind admire her that we disgrace her in any other, but let all her wayes be according unto their place and degree adored.' It is here that we must assert the second main element in classical Anglicanism, the traditionalist view. Tradition is something handed on, but that way of putting it makes it sound rather static, whereas the reality is dynamic. Traditionalists, to revert to the astronomical metaphor, believe in 'continuous creation', believe that God is dynamically active in guiding his Church and that Christian truth is something that continues to unfold. But there is no real disjunction between biblicism and traditionalism. Historians of the canon of Scripture tell us that the formation of the New Testament was not completed until the fourth century, so the very process of authenticating the canonical books is itself a part of tradition, of that process of guidance into the truth. Nevertheless, the canon of Scripture being closed, a useful distinction, though not an absolute one, can be made between the two approaches.

The traditionalist tends to see the Church as the place of revelation, with the Bible, created by the Church, as a normative element, but only an element in that dynamic tradition. The traditionalist will point to the Councils of the Church that produced the great christological and trinitarian doctrines as an obvious example of this dynamic process. It is true that everything they formulated was found implicitly declared in Scripture, but there was a large leap from the simple and inchoate creeds of the New Testament to the fully articulated doctrines of the Council of Chalcedon in 451, for example. While it is true that all things necessary to salvation are already found in Scripture, they were so given that Christians were not explicitly conscious of all their intellectual implications until subsequently defined. John Henry Newman was the greatest recent exponent of this dynamic view of Christian doctrine. He summarized his position as follows:

> It is well known that, though the creed of the Church has been one and the same from the beginning, yet it has been so deeply lodged in her bosom as to be held by individuals more or less implicitly instead of being delivered from the first in those special statements, or what are called definitions, under which it is now presented to us, and which preclude mistake or ignorance. These definitions which are but the expression of portions of the one dogma which has ever been received by the Church, are the work of time; they have grown to their present shape and number in the course of eighteen centuries, under the exigency of successive events, such as heresies and the like, and they may of course receive still further additions as time goes on. Now this process of doctrinal development, as you might suppose, is not of an accidental or random character, it is conducted upon laws, as everything else which comes from God; and the study of its laws and of its exhibition, or, in other words, the science and history of the formation of theology, was a subject which had interested me more than anything else from the time I first began to read the Fathers, and which had engaged my attention in a special way.*

Many Anglicans would disagree with the scope Newman gave to his theory of Development, but his general outline of it provides us with an interpretation of the role of Church and tradition in the unfolding or explication of revealed truth that many Anglicans would agree with. But the argument does not only refer to the development and definition of essential truth. Hooker would maintain that it applies, with even greater vigour, to the legitimate development of forms and customs that are

*Wilfrid Ward, *The Life of John Henry, Cardinal Newman*, vol. 1, p. 186.

useful, though not essential to salvation, the point being that many things can edify Christians, under the guidance of the Holy Spirit working through human reason, that are not directly deducible from, or absolutely authenticated by, Scripture. This is an insight that cuts both ways. There are essential developments, definitions that are explications of the original *deposit*, and there are legitimate and useful developments that do not bear this essential character. The biblicist tends to repudiate these developments, because they are not directly deducible from Scripture, but the traditionalist often makes the opposite mistake, by elevating secondary matters to the primary level, by assuming that matters of discipline and polity, for instance, come within the enclosure of necessary faith. In Book iii of his *Of the Laws of Ecclesiastical Politie* Hooker refuted the Puritan contention that 'in Scripture there must be of necessitie contained a forme of Church-politie the lawes whereof may in no wise be altered'. It was Hooker's contention, and I believe a correct one, that forms of polity were matters of discipline, not of faith, and that considerable local differences could be allowed. I believe that a dose of Hooker's judicious wisdom would be the best guide through the current debate about the admission of women to Holy Orders.

If the biblicists have made the revelation too narrow and the Traditionalists have made it too wide, it has been the function of the liberal or rationalist element in Anglicanism to criticize the excesses and enthusiasms of both of them. This is an important and necessary function, but it is essentially a corrective upon excessive definition rather than anything definite in itself. It is usually easier to discover what it opposes, in matters of central doctrine, rather than what it proposes. Most of the things liberals are in favour of come within the rubric of second-order truths, and many of them I would agree with, but the certainty with which they espouse these secondary or derivative matters is in marked contrast to their uncertainty in the face of the central doctrines of Christianity. One can always tell where liberals stand on the ordination of women or the role of the Church in politics or the proper freedom of academics to pursue their researches into Christian origins; it is usually much harder to discover what they mean when they come to discuss the incarnation or the resurrection. We know, of course, that they do not accept the Virgin birth or the empty tomb, but what they do accept is never exactly clear.

My own theory about the liberal principle in Anglicanism is twofold. I believe, first of all, that it is a reflection of the sociological imprisonment of Anglicanism in the West today among the educated middle class. This is a group that is particularly exposed to the prevailing winds of intellectual fashion, and a relativizing scepticism is the norm in these circles today. Something which T. S. Eliot wrote in 1948 has proved prophetic.

'One of the features of development, whether we are taking the religious or the cultural point of view, is the appearance of scepticism – by which, of course, I do not mean infidelity or destructiveness (still less the unbelief which is due to mental sloth) but the habit of examining evidence and the capacity for delayed decision. Scepticism is a highly civilized trait, though, when it declines into pyrrhonism,* it is one of which civilization can die. Where scepticism is strength, pyrrhonism is weakness: for we need not only the strength to defer a decision, but the strength to make one.'†

I believe that there are many signs in the West today that we are in the grip of the pyrrhonism that Eliot saw as the dissolvent of civilization. I feel the influence of it in myself; I do not always know where a healthy and important scepticism ends and the erosion of absolute scepticism begins, but I suspect we are well into it in the West today in a number of important areas. One of the things that seems to happen at that stage of cultural disintegration is that the vacuum left by the erosion of objective standards and values is filled by fashionable causes, and dogma is replaced by chic, radical and otherwise. It is not exactly easy to see what can be done about this situation, but a beginning might be made by applying scepticism to scepticism and bringing a little more humility to bear on our investigations into the tradition.

But I also believe that this very scepticism, with all its dangers, is an essential element in a healthy community that has a concern

*The doctrine of the impossibility of attaining certainty of knowledge; absolute scepticism.
†*Notes towards the Definition of Culture*, p. 29.

for truth. We need constantly to interrogate our assumptions and examine our convictions, if we are to remain honest and open to the spirit of truth. We need, above all, to recognize that there is a hierarchy of truth and that some things can be left to private judgement, while others have to be held to by the whole body if Christian doctrine is to have any coherence and efficacy. We will rarely learn what to believe to our soul's health from liberals, therefore, but listening to them may help us to sift the unnecessary chaff from the pure wheat, and most of us carry too much chaff in our knapsack.

If the tragic thing about Anglicanism is that it is a house divided, the miraculous thing about it is that each of the divisions in the household is uncannily adapted to correct and balance the others, and in a rough and ready way this correcting and balancing already goes on. My longing for the Anglican Church is for this rather haphazard process to become intentional, though as I write the words I realize that such planning may be foreign to the muddled genius of Anglicanism. It may be wrong to contrive an internal ecumenism formally, but I continue to hope it may happen informally and naturally as members of each faction listen to and are influenced by the others. I dare say people will continue to stomp away from the Anglican Church in disgust, and it is as well to recognize that to sustain membership in the Church requires a particular kind of patience and a distinctive sense of humour. For those of us who can sustain the dust and the tumult there are peculiar rewards, the most conspicuous being an almost total absence of boredom as we comtemplate the extraordinary antics of our brothers and sisters. Anglicanism in one sense exists only as an idea, a synthesis of types, each of which is defective in itself but powerfully effective when united with its opposites. It could be argued that this synthesis has not yet happened in Anglicanism, or that it has to go on happening all the time because the tensions never cease. Whatever be the truth of the matter, it is not an easy Church to belong to, but we are not, anyway, meant to be at ease in Zion. We may not be at ease, but we do have our moments of enormous joy as we relish the absurdity of our own existence. Only God could sustain such an impossibility in being, and G. K. Chesterton may help us to understand why:

Joy, which was the small publicity of the pagan, is the gigantic secret of the Christian. And as I close this chaotic volume I open again the strange small book from which all Christianity came; and I am again haunted by a kind of confirmation. The tremendous figure which fills the Gospels towers in this respect, as in every other, above all the thinkers who ever thought themselves tall. His pathos was natural, almost casual. The Stoics, ancient and modern, were proud of concealing their tears. He never concealed His tears; He showed them plainly on His open face at any daily sight, such as the far sight of His native city. Yet he concealed something. Solemn supermen and imperial diplomatists are proud of restraining their anger. He never restrained His Anger. He flung furniture down the front steps of the Temple, and asked men how they expected to escape the damnation of Hell. Yet He restrained something. I say it with reverence; there was in that shattering personality a thread that must be called shyness. There was something that He hid from all men when He went up a mountain to pray. There was something that He covered constantly by abrupt silence or impetuous isolation. There was some one thing that was too great for God to show us when He walked upon our earth; and I have sometimes fancied that it was His mirth.*

*_Orthodoxy_, p. 296.

# Glory Broken

Christians are people of a book, people for whom words are important, people for whom words convey wordless realities, express, in a way, the inexpressible, seek to utter the unutterable. Words are important to us, though they conceal as much as they reveal. Words, like music, can tantalize us almost to madness, for they promise and promise and yet they neither fail us nor completely fulfil us. We are never quite held in the ecstasy by language, taken fully out of ourselves for ever. Grey reality rolls back over us, yet who would give up the precious moment, 'the moment in the rose garden', the sudden glimpse, the startled realization? Words have extraordinary power. There is what Eliot called 'the word within a word', the voice behind the thing written or spoken that answers to some other voice within us. That is why stray phrases, taken out of context, have enormous power to move us at a level below or above mere thought. Shakespeare's writings are full of these phrases, words that halt us and sweep some emotion right through us: 'We have heard the chimes at midnight', says Falstaff to Master Shallow, and we are engulfed with a strange and immediate sense of loss and joyful remembrance at the same time. There are phrases in T. S. Eliot's writings that leap out in the same way, causing us to look up suddenly and put the book down for a moment: 'In the juvescence of the year came Christ the tiger.' And, of course, *the* book, the Bible itself, is full of these words within a word. Every Holy Week I wait for four short words from John's Gospel. Judas, we are told, had just left the upper room, 'and it was night'.

Recently in my reading I came across two passages that halted me and made me think, because they caught on to something not quite formed in my own musings on the meaning of life. The first is an aphorism from V. V. Rozanov: 'All religions will pass, but this will remain: simply sitting in a chair and looking into the distance.' What do we see when we sit in that chair and look into the distance? I think we see two things contending, and the question life brings is whether they are reconciled in some sense, or whether one simply overcomes the other. The two things that contend are well expressed in the other passage I read, this time from Cyril Connolly's *The Unquiet Grave*: 'There are two ways to be a great writer. One way is like Homer, Shakespeare and Goethe to accept life completely, the other (Pascal's, Proust's, Leopardi's, Baudelaire's) is to refuse ever to lose sight of its horror. One must be Prospero or Caliban; in between lie vast dissipated areas of pleasure and weakness.' Connolly, of course, applied the distinction to writers, but that does not preclude us from borrowing the dualism and applying it more widely. Literature reflects life as much as it interprets it, so we should expect it to mirror what we see and understand of life.

So there are two things the man sees from that chair; or it may be better to say that what he sees has a double effect upon him. I wish to reverse Connolly's order and to lay my first emphasis upon the refusal ever to lose sight of life's horror. I fully accept that most of us live, not on the edges of greatness, but in what Connolly calls 'the vast dissipated areas of pleasure and weakness' that lie in between. Humankind cannot bear very much reality, so we find all sorts of ways of occupying or distracting our attention from the contemplation of the meaning or meaninglessness of life. Just as there are few great writers so there are few of us who can really concentrate on reality and its horrors, so occasions must be sought when we bring ourselves back to attention, when we sit in that chair and start looking into the distance. Sometimes what we see is a horror of meaninglessness. 'The eternal silence of these infinite spaces terrifies me', says Pascal, and we know what he means. I am equally terrified by the vast spaces of human history, the sheer weight of the numbers of humanity oppresses me, the thought, not only of all the people there are, but of all the people there ever were numbs me into a kind of stupefaction, especially since most of them have had but a short time to live and were full of misery. Only a tiny percentage of any generation in history has achieved more than a fleeting moment of earthly consolation, and we must not let our own exceptional experience obscure this truth from our eyes. During the last forty years in the West the economic successes of various types of welfare capitalism have spread some of the advantages of wealth throughout the population in a way previously unknown in history and still largely unknown in the rest of the world today. Wealth brings the consolation of leisure (and its unavoidable concomitant, boredom) and it removes the crushing burden of drudgery, the endless struggle to stay in the same place, to eat, be warm, find shelter. These are still matters of daily struggle to most people on earth, and they were to us until within living memory. I am, for instance, haunted by the story of my grandmother, my mother's mother, whom I never knew. She lived her short life in the tenements of Maryhill in Glasgow. My grandfather, her first husband, died when my mother was four, and she married a private in the Highland Light Infantry, a famous Glasgow regiment of 'wee hard men'. While he was away with the army she struggled to raise five children in the slums of Glasgow, and it was obviously too much for her. The details of her life and death are vague, but my mother told me that when she was eight my grandmother was brought home one afternoon on a coalcart, having dropped dead in the street, after some years of addiction to methylated spirits. All the children were sent off to orphanages and never really lived together as a family again.

When I was ordained I went back to work in the slums of Glasgow, just before they knocked them all down and replaced them with the famously inhuman 'multi-storeys'. I could still sense what it must have been like to have been intensely poor in my grandmother's day. Sometimes I got a sense of it all, both the pride of it, the struggle and the love, as well as the defeat. My mother inherited something from it, a deep insecurity and sadness allied to a tigerish loyalty to her children and an ability to work and struggle for them in a way that still overwhelms me. She took two jobs, one scrubbing floors and one in a fruit shop, to pay for my fare to Kelham Theological College when I was sent there at fourteen. Sitting in that chair and looking into the distance fills one with an enormous sorrowing and pride at the way human beings struggle to survive and care for their young in the face of what often seems to be a pitiless universe. That is still the lot of most people today on the face of the earth, but that is a sort of passive horror, a pity at watching people adapt to and finally be overwhelmed by a merciless desert. There are, however, worse horrors to contemplate. Human beings seem to have a genius for misery, so that when we no longer have to struggle against the external constraints of poverty and disease we turn the conflict inward and tear ourselves apart. The psychic torments of the affluent, with their unsatisfied longings and broken relationships and the enormous disappointment many of them feel about life in their fifth decade, is, in its way, quite as acute as any other kind of misery, but even that is far from the last word on the subject. Let us return to the man sitting in the chair, looking into the distance.

Rozanov, in the aphorism already quoted, said that 'all religions will pass, but this will remain: simply sitting in a chair and looking into the distance'. I would invert what he said and claim that religion will endure as long as a man sits in a chair looking into the distance, because it is from the distance, from the beyond that surrounds us, that revelations come; meaning, or its opposite, is disclosed. We have to contemplate life, study it, wait for it, before it yields its meaning and that meaning is not necessarily one that will comfort us. Just as the way people have had to live can be a desolating thing to contemplate, so can a perception of the inner meaning of life be equally depressing. We tend to think of religion as a comforting thing, an opiate, but it is probably truer to say that most religions are frightening, their vision horrifies more than it consoles. Something in the universe communicates itself to us as hostile, demanding, implacable and ultimately unappeasable. I want to call that bleak recognition 'Law' and I want to go back to the Old Testament to try to understand it.

Reading in the Book of Numbers one morning I was suddenly overwhelmed by an enormous sense of the sheer petulance of the God Moses contended with on behalf of the people of Israel. The incident occurred in chapter eleven where the people started weeping as they remembered the food they had eaten in Egypt, with its varied diet of fish and cucumbers, melons and leeks, while all they had to eat in the wilderness was coriander seed. Moses brings the complaint to God, who replies: 'The Lord will give you meat, and you shall eat. You shall not eat one day, or two days, or five days, or ten days, or twenty days, but a whole month, until it comes out at your nostrils and becomes loathsome to you, because you have rejected the Lord who is among you, and have wept before him, saying, "Why did we come forth out of Egypt?" ' (Numbers 11:19). Whether we think all religion is human projection or divine revelation mixed up with our mistaken apprehension of it, passages such as this raise interesting issues. There is no doubt that the God revealed to Moses is angry much of the time and Moses frequently intercedes on behalf of the people of Israel to fend off some act of divine revenge. Moses is often successful. God, we read, 'repents of his anger' and spares the delinquents, though just as often his wrath leaps out against them. The Old Testament is full of visitations of divine wrath, smiting with fire, pestilence and sword. And standing firmly in the middle is the man Moses, repelled and fascinated by the Lord, driven to anger and to tenderness by the rabble he leads, seeking to interpret the one to the other. I do not think we can make confident judgements about the history or theology of this remote period, but something begins to emerge from it all, a vision that makes Moses and his achievement and experience an emblem that represents a certain perception of reality. In an important and significant encounter with God, Moses makes a request: ' "I pray thee, show me thy glory." But, he said, "you cannot see my face; for man shall not see me and live." And the Lord said, "Behold, there is a place by me where you shall stand upon the rock; and while my glory passes by I will put you in a cleft of the rock, and I will cover you with my hand until I have passed by; then I will take away my hand, and you shall see my back; but my face shall not be seen" ' (Exodus 33:18, 20–23).

The word translated 'glory' in this passage has a complicated history. The basic meaning of the Greek word used to translate the Hebrew is 'expectation, view, opinion', gradually evolving to 'conjecture, repute, praise, fame'. This Greek word 'doxa' (found, for instance, in our word 'orthodoxy', meaning 'right belief'), is used to translate the Old Testament concept of kabod, glory, honour. When it is used of God it refers, not to God's essential nature, but to what we can see, what is manifested to us, what is revealed to us. If a person reveals his doxa to me, I capture something of his real personality and nature, something of the inner person flashes forth for me. God's doxa is the luminous manifestation of his person, the glorious revelation of himself. When we contemplate the universe and ask, 'Show me thy glory', we are wanting to know what it means, what its real nature is; we want some signal or message from the distance, some reflected glory, something that will flash back an answer to us. Religion is full of claims of signals received, messages delivered, glory revealed, but the perplexing thing about religion is that we can never know for sure whether we are receiving messages or projecting them, whether there is a real revelation from the distance back to us, or whether it is our own fears and longings that bounce back at us from the great, empty screen overhead. I do not want to linger over that irresolvable debate, however, because Moses provides us with a good example of a type of religion that hardly flatters its adherents. It is significant that Moses is only allowed to see God's back, not his face; not his full glory, but a luminous shadow sweeping round the corner. God turns his back to Moses and it is this sense of radical aversion that comes through the religion he founded. Remember Connolly's words about a resolute determination not to lose sight of the horror of life and we may have a clue to the turbulent and enigmatic religious movement started by Moses. Moses stands for Law, the attempt to order and arrange the unhappy multitude. Law is the inevitable reaction of the compassionate and enraged man who gazes out at the complicated miseries of humanity. 'The law was given through Moses', the Fourth Evangelist tells us. Moses represents the attempt to make sense of the universe by imposing order upon it. The God with whom Moses wrestles is a wrathful believer in law and order, driven to furious outbursts of rage against the people whom he unwisely created and their incurable weaknesses. The thing that breaks the heart of Moses is his identification with both parties in the endless dispute, the controversy that God has with Israel. He clearly has enormous sympathy with the people he leads and he wrestles with the strange fact that they are created sick, yet commanded to be sound by God. Whether all this is a projection of human struggle onto that distant screen we gaze at, or a genuine reflection back to us of something profoundly disturbed in the very heart of reality, the effect is the same. It brings into history the experience of unappeasable demand and irremovable guilt. Hell is created. On the one hand we have a Divine Judge who has established his universe on rational principles of law and, on the other hand, we have creatures who are commanded to obey that law on pain of eternal perdition, yet who find in themselves a tragic resistance to the law, and a mysterious compulsion to court their own ruin. Human creatures find themselves in the excruciating dilemma: 'Created sick, commanded to be sound'. God is experienced as Demand, he becomes the Enemy who wants the world to run like a detention centre, and this external picture of reality and meaning is imposed upon our inner nature as guilt.

How fertile guilt has been in the history of our culture! An article in the *New York Times* of 11 September 1984 put an interesting modern angle on the ancient problem. The article was about Dr Joan Harvey's psychological research on the sense many people have that they are fakes. 'Dr Harvey was among several psychologists and therapists whose findings led them to conclude that many achievers feel they are fakes and imposters and live in terror of being exposed as the frauds they really are. The article discusses case after case of very bright high achievers in all fields who suffer from fear that others would discover their own sense of low self-esteem. This is called "the imposter phenomenon": no matter how secure you may appear to be, and no matter how high and successful you are, or even how lowly and modest you are, at heart most of us have moments of extreme anxiety about our real place in the scheme of things, and the characteristic nature of this anxiety is secrecy. Dr Harvey feels that the sense of fraudulence is so fundamental, so basic, that most people assume it is the natural state of things and would never think to discuss it or acknowledge it; thus, like some psychic cancer, it gnaws at our vitals, and the only release is death.'* But even death brings its own anxiety, for after death is the real judgement when the secrets of all hearts will be disclosed, when God will open the books on us and really expose in the harsh light what we have known all along in the darkness of our own secret guilt.

The irony is, of course, that a culture based on fear, guilt and the radical interiorization of a sense of profound failure becomes

*Peter Gomes, from a sermon preached at Harvard University on 9 December 1984.

a truly horrifying civilization. And this horror operates on various levels. There is, for instance, the horrible effect that guilt and repression build into the unconscious mind of whole generations, erupting in orgies of hate and persecution. The most devastating example in history is the Holocaust, the systematic attempt to exterminate the Jewish community in Germany – and German-occupied countries. That is a horror so fraught with meaning and bristling with so many implications for theology and politics that it seems almost blasphemous to mention it almost in passing, but if we are engaged in a determined effort not to lose sight of the horror of life, then we cannot afford to ignore the most obscene incident in human history, in our own era, certainly one of the grimmest eras in recorded time. George Steiner in his meditation on the Holocaust sees it as a great act of vengeance against God and the morality of demand, to both of which the Jews have witnessed for millennia. We have not yet come to terms with the Holocaust, perhaps we never shall, but we ought not to blink at the horror of it. Let me offer a single snapshot, from Treblinka. Treblinka was an extermination camp in Poland where thousands of Jews were gassed by the Nazis, sometimes as many as 18,000 a day. They came by train from Warsaw. As soon as they arrived at the station they were told to undress and take a shower. Then the gas was turned on. Trainload after trainload later filled the pits at Treblinka with corpses. The Nazis kept a squad of Jewish slaves to clear out the gas chambers and bury the bodies; until they went mad or killed themselves. Few survived Treblinka. One who did has captured the horror of it all in one paragraph. He describes how the Jewish slaves had to open the doors of the gas chambers and drag the corpses to the mass graves. He goes on: 'Sometimes we found living children among the warm bodies. Little children, still alive, clinging to their mothers' bodies. We strangled them with our own hands before throwing them into the grave.' The gas ovens and extermination camps of the Third Reich bear a strange resemblance to the fully detailed picture of hell that gradually evolved in the Christian tradition, and I do not believe the resemblance is accidental. Centuries of guilt and dread stoked the boilers of the Holocaust, so that God's ancient people, the Jews, who for two thousand years never bore arms and never had either missionary empires or coloured slaves, might be banished from the earth. The 'Final Solution' is the realized eschatology of the doctrine of hell.

The deepest irony lies in the fact that behind the worst excesses of history is usually found a commitment, either conscious or unconscious, to side with God in re-ordering his universe. Wars are fought by *believers*, confident of their mission to cure society of its ills. Though most current examples come from the creeds of Mohammed and Marx, Christian history is full of examples of the same overweening urge to impose virtue on individuals and societies. One of the greatest philosophical texts of this century is an attack upon this sort of totalitarianism. In *The Open Society and Its Enemies* Karl Popper showed that at the heart of the thought of the three most influential political thinkers in history – Plato, Hegel and Marx – lay the same totalitarian urge to impose pattern and order, their kind of order, upon recalcitrant human beings. These are the great archetypal enemies of the open society whose 'virtues' have done more damage to human happiness than most vices put together. H. L. Mencken captured the paradox nicely: 'The worst government is the most moral. One composed of cynics is often very tolerant and humane. But when fanatics are on top there is no limit to oppression'.*

Sitting in that chair, looking into the distance, refusing to lose sight of life's horror, we are overwhelmed by the paradox of Law. The penal view of the universe, the perception of it as a great testing ground for eternity, seems to rebound upon it, visiting its children with the very penalties they sought to avoid, building into them a guilt they cannot assuage, a sense of demand they cannot appease and a fatal longing for order that can only be satisfied by the exaction of a terrible price. The most apt contemporary symbol of our predicament is the nuclear bomb. Possession of The Bomb is a form of absolute security that threatens us with absolute destruction. We dare not use it, yet dare not renounce it. It is the final expression of the essentially pyrrhic nature of the human struggle: we are destroyed by our own victories, corrupted by our own virtues. So contemplating human history sometimes fills us with anger. We can understand the wrath of God, his sheer exasperation at the self-destructive irrationality of human beings. Yet it can be argued that it is that

*Notebooks, *Minority Report*, p. 327.

very anger that deranges men and women, giving them a sense that they are always being tested and found wanting, 'created sick, commanded to be sound'. The Christian homosexual is an emblem of this particular dilemma. He finds himself, through no conscious act, nothing to which he has given consent, born against the grain of the universe, and to the loneliness which any member of a permanent minority feels is added a burden of guilt and self-loathing that often leads to despair. And this is the poor wretch with whom God contends! It is scarcely surprising that many of the most sensitive people in history have refused to co-operate with such a God or such a universe. Like Ivan Kara-mazov, they return the ticket and refuse to take part in the show. God's wrath kindles man's anger and the controversy resounds in history.

But what if a profound mistake has been made? Is it possible that we have misunderstood God or given too much emphasis to one aspect of his revealed nature? Is there, perhaps, a conflict within the Godhead, a struggle within the divine nature that shows itself in the contradictions of revelation, that incarnates itself in the person of Christ? However we put it we are faced with a paradox, the same paradox that Connolly noted in the obsessions of the great writers: the choice between rejection and acceptance. Whether we are projecting this struggle onto God or receiving it from God, or whether it is a little of both, the question is the same: how is the struggle resolved? There *is* a struggle, a conflict of interpretations of the universe and understandings of God. We have seen the dark side of God, his back turned towards us in anger. In Connolly's phrase, we have refused to lose sight of the horror of life. But there is another way of looking at life, another thing to contemplate as we sit in that chair and gaze into the distance. The paradox is well expressed in the proverb: 'The young man cries for justice; the old man cries for mercy.' Anger and the law's demands are young virtues, bred of that intolerance that does not yet know its own limits and frailties. Mercy, on the other hand, is a mellow and wistful virtue, bred of failure and the knowledge that all things are no longer possible. Mercy is conspicuous in Shakespeare, the man who accepted life completely and chronicled its follies and frailties with compassion.

> Therefore, Jew,
> Though justice be thy plea, consider this –
> That in the course of justice none of us
> Should see salvation; we do pray for mercy,
> And that same prayer doth teach us all to render
> The deeds of mercy.*

This sort of compassionate realism is often found in poets, playwrights and novelists who are intimately familiar with human nature, whereas it is less common among moralists and professional students of religion, who are usually more familiar with abstract ideas. But there is a rumour in history, strongly reflected in Scripture, that God, by reputation harsh and perfectionist in his response to human weakness, actually understands our condition, knows whereof we are made, remembers that we are but dust, and gives us an eternity in which to improve. A. S. J. Tessimond, in a thoughtfully subversive poem, *Heaven*, celebrates the rumour:

> In the heaven of the god I hope for (call him X)
> There is marriage and giving in marriage and transient sex
> For those who will cast the body's vest aside
> Soon, but are not yet wholly rarefied
> And still embrace. For X is never annoyed
> Or shocked; has read his Jung and knows his Freud,
> He gives you time in heaven to do as you please,
> To climb love's gradual ladder by slow degrees
> Gently to rise from sense to soul, to ascend
> To a world of timeless joy, world without end.
>
> Here on the gates of pearl there hangs no sign
> Limiting cakes and ale, forbidding wine.
> No weakness here is hidden, no vice unknown.
> Sin is a sickness to be cured, outgrown.
> With the help of a god who can laugh, an unsolemn god
> Who smiles at old wives' tale of iron rod
> And fiery hell, a god who's more at ease
> With bawds and Falstaffs than with pharisees.
>
> Here the lame learn to leap, the blind to see.

*The Merchant of Venice*, Act 4, Scene 1

Tyrants are taught to be humble, slaves to be free.
Fools become wise, and wise men cease to be bores,
Here bishops learn from lips of back-street whores,
And white men follow black-faced angels' feet
Through fields of orient and immortal wheat.

Villon, Lautrec and Baudelaire are here.
Here Swift forgets his anger, Poe his fear.
Napoleon rests. Columbus, journeys done,
Has reached his new Atlantis, found his sun.
Verlaine and Dylan Thomas drink together.
Marx talks to Plato. Byron wonders whether
There's some mistake. Wordsworth has found a hill
That's home. Here Chopin plays the piano still.
Wren plans ethereal domes; and Renoir paints
Young girls as ripe as fruit but not yet saints.

And X, of whom no coward is afraid,
Who's friend consulted, not fierce king obeyed;
Who hears the unspoken thought, the prayer unprayed;
Who expects not even the learned to understand
His universe, extends a prodigal hand,
Full of forgiveness, over his promised land.

Part of the enigma of Christ lies in the fact that we seem to find in him absolute harshness and absolute tenderness, complete rejection and complete acceptance. I am repelled and mystified by Christ, yet I am inescapably drawn to him, feel that here I am really understood and forgiven. His harshness, the petulant blasting of the barren fig tree, the denunciatory Christ of the Fourth Gospel, all upset me, in much the same way as the bad-tempered God of the Old Testament upsets me; yet his understanding towards sinners, the low company he kept and his obvious fondness for women in a culture that did not regard them very highly, all fill me with hope. What I am looking for is absolute acceptance, just as I am, because I know I am probably not going to change. I do not entirely understand the source of my own weaknesses and longings, and part of me wants to be condemned for them, but I have found people in my life who have accepted me utterly, who have given me the grace of loving me even in what I think of as my sins, and I need to know if

God does that. Is his love for me absolute and unconditional, or must I qualify for it? It seems to me that there has been a psychological contradiction in the answer that has been given by the Christian tradition. Christianity invented hell and used it to keep people good. There was conduct that led to hell and eternal damnation, and there was the narrow way that led to life eternal. Even if the idea of hell is not used as empirically as it once was, there is still a strong tradition of penal deterrence in Christianity, a kind of balance of guilt and terror designed to keep us in control. Many theologians have quietly expunged that from the tradition and given us, instead, a modern, non-judgemental God, modelled on current social-work theory. I cannot easily accept that truncated view of the Christian revelation, because it means that a strong element in the tradition, expressed by Christ, certainly taught by the early Church and believed down the ages, has been arbitrarily removed either because it is uncomfortable or because it does not fit with the modern view of behavioural science. I cannot remove the horror that way, by turning in the chair and looking away. It is there in front of me, it is inside me, it is in centuries of Christian struggle, that awful demand made by God that I behave myself or go to hell.

> Lo! the book exactly worded,
>   Wherein all hath been recorded,
>   Thence shall judgement be awarded.
>
> When the judge his seat attaineth,
>   And each hidden deed arraigneth,
>   Nothing unavenged remaineth.
>
> What shall I, frail man, be pleading?
>   Who for me be interceding,
>   When the just are mercy needing?

It is useless to try to expunge all that from the tradition, just as it is useless to turn your eyes away from the crimes and follies of humanity. We cannot banish that trumpet note from Scripture; it summons us to dread.

> Wondrous sound the trumpet flingeth,
>   Through earth's sepulchres it ringeth,
>   All before the throne it bringeth.

Death is struck, and nature quaking,
　All creation is awaking,
　To its judge an answer making.*

That note is there all right, and it would make Christianity an easier religion to understand if it were the only note. Christianity would then be a moralistic religion like many others, designed to inculcate high standards of behaviour, to defer immediate gratifications for the sake of larger ones kept in store for us. Christianity would then be a sort of moral monetarism: discipline today and the rewards of virtue some other day. Of course, Christianity has been made to conform to that pattern; it is what many people think Christianity is. It has its successes as well as its casualties, though it probably has more of the latter, because many people, perhaps most people, cannot help themselves, cannot change, cannot learn to defer gratification, cannot, in short, obey the law. These are the ones who are reduced to despair by the law's demands. They may consent to the law with their mind, acknowledge that it would be far, far better were they able to keep it, but they know another part of them does not and cannot consent to the law. If salvation is by law, then they are cursed.

The unresolved contradiction in Christian doctrine emerges because all that is, apparently, recognized by God. He knows that we have no power of ourselves to help ourselves so, it is said, he freely gives what he commands. He accepts us absolutely. He declares us righteous and sound, though we are and know ourselves to be neither. The trouble is that this note of absolute, unconditional grace, does not obliterate the other. Paul is the great celebrant of God's unmerited grace; he is the great analyst of the failure of law to make and keep us good; he offers us absolute forgiveness, joyous absolution; but then he seems to take it away, fearful of its effect upon us, and back come the warnings, the excommunications, the lists of sins that will deny us access to the grace he has already told us is ours while we are yet sinners. So Christian doctrine becomes a sort of torture, an unresolved contradiction. Are we saved absolutely in spite of our sins, forgiven by the mercy of a God who loves us to the uttermost? Is that why the message is called good news? Or is it all a cruel

*Dies Irae*, English Hymnal, 351.

word game, a sort of divine teasing, in which we are offered gifts and then have them snatched back until we have cleaned up our act? What is the right message, what *is* reflected back to us from that ancient glory? And it is no use telling me that both are still there, because it is not possible to live with that contradiction unresolved. I have to know whether I have to work out my own salvation (or, more likely, damnation), or whether I am saved. I have to know whether all those New Testament metaphors mean anything when they tell me I am ransomed, redeemed, justified, accepted, or whether they are only a new kind of carrot to get me trotting faster.

I think the contradiction is resolved, but it is a resolution that is dangerous, so dangerous that the saints and theologians have tried to protect God from it, just as Peter tried to protect Christ from his own determination to suffer. We have asked God to show us his glory. We have looked into the distance and seen two principles contending, in history, in God's relations with his ancient people the Jews, and in the life of Christ: law and grace, condemnation and absolution, absolute abandonment or absolute care. Christ never resolves them in words. His words seem to come in blocks of contradiction: on the one hand are the warnings about the ease with which we can suffer absolute loss, and on the other hand are the assurances about the father who is home to us after all our wanderings and who rushes to meet us while we are yet far off. He raises the level of demand to an absolute pitch; he promulgates a law that condemns us for our very thoughts and unbidden impulses; he commands the impossible with a beauty and a passion that makes us affirm it and long for it, even as we know it is utterly beyond our reach. He perplexes his disciples; he angers the leaders of his people; the only ones who derive comfort from him are the ones who seem furthest from his impossible ideal, the harlots and tax-gatherers. Then he stops speaking. The contradictions remain suspended in the air, unresolved. He does not offer an explanation or resolve the paradox he has created. We are told only that he suddenly set his face towards Jerusalem and went to his death; and that death was the answer to our question because it is called by John his glorification. Glory, we have seen, is what we catch of the nature of God, it is the shining of his being into our eyes, it is his self-disclosure, the showing of his face. We have strained to see that glory, catch that message, read, from the distance, the meaning of time, and this is what we are given: the crucifixion of Christ, who called it his glorification, the place where the mind of God is made plain. What does it mean? In Elie Wiesel's novel about the Holocaust, *Night*, we watch the murder and torture of the innocent, the martyrdom of faith itself, as a child watches the hanging of another child and asks: ' "Where is God? Where is he?" . . . And I heard a voice within me answer: "Where is he? Here he is – he is hanging here on this gallows".' That is the only answer that can justify God, and it is the meaning of the cross. The cross is the sign of that contradiction that besets us. On the cross Christ embraced the contradiction, resolved it by bearing it, dying in it. In a mysterious phrase Paul says that the cross cancelled the bill humanity had run up. Christ simply took it away. But the cross only means anything because it is God who is shown at work in it; that is the glory we see in it, the meaning of it from that distance we call God. 'Where is God? Where is he?', we ask, and we hear a voice within us answer: 'Where is God? Here he is – he is hanging here on this cross.'

What cannot be resolved by logic or amendment of life God in silence bears, simply takes away. To speak in metaphor, he consumes his own anger, pays the debts of the children he created but cannot control, assumes absolute responsibility. What he has done is completely contrary to all human prudence and wisdom. He has acted with the intoxicated passion of a lover who disregards every convention in his commitment to the beloved. God's salvation, his tearing up of the great moral bond that is held against us, lies at the heart of the Christian gospel, like a buried mine. It is an outrageous and dangerous doctrine and it is not surprising that the Church has never fully come to terms with it, because it shows us a God whose glory is shown in suffering. The glory that is reflected back to us from the infinite silence we look into is the broken glory of the crucified God. Nothing else works, apparently, not even hell. What we cannot earn; what we cannot be scared into; what we cannot contrive by our own intelligence, God freely grants us. It is not surprising that a doctrine so scandalous should be suppressed by organized Christianity, because it is revolutionary in its impact. It reduces us all to the same level: sinners, yet justified, but always sinners.

King of majesty tremendous,
    Who dost free salvation send us,
    Fount of pity, then befriend us.

In a universe in which God has been crucified for us all, we dare not, can no longer afford to despise anyone.